A memoir by *Emory Easton*

Mother, can you hear me now?

Woodhall Press
Norwalk, CT

Mother, can you hear me now?

A memoir by

Emory Easton

Woodhall Press
Norwalk, CT

woodhall press

Woodhall Press, 81 Old Saugatuck Road, Norwalk, CT 06855
WoodhallPress.com

Copyright © 2021 Emory Easton

Cover design: Asha Hossain
Layout artist: Wendy Bowes

Library of Congress Cataloging-in-Publication Data available

ISBN 978-1-949116-49-6 (paper: alk paper)
ISBN 978-1-949116-60-1 (electronic)

First Edition

Distributed by Independent Publishers Group
(800) 888-4741

Printed in the United States of America

This book came about as a cathartic exercise. It healed me of my past and made me "whole" for the first time.

This book is dedicated to people have endured verbal, sexual, physical abuse. It proves you can find your voice and be a better part of yourself.

Contents

CHAPTER	PAGE

CHAPTER 1

Secrets

I sat in the living room while my mother, Elise, lay on the couch, an oxygen mask pulled away from her face so she could smoke a cigarette.

She was dying, with less than three months to live.

I was forty-two years old and I needed answers.

It turned out my mother needed to talk as much as I needed to listen. She began to cry as she confessed to being a terrible mother, saying that she was so sorry. I didn't know if I could forgive her. I was waiting to hear her story first.

My mom asked me, "When does life begin? Conception? Birth? Or somewhere in between?"

I didn't know the answer.

She continued. "I made you a survivor. You've always landed on your feet."

Mom shared my birth story with me for the first time.

She and my biological dad, John, had separated when Mom found out she was pregnant. He denied I was his child and insisted he owed my mom nothing. Mom said he had already found someone else.

She stopped for a moment to look around at the threadbare carpet and the walls with their peeling plaster and paint that was puke-green, and then she started to sob.

Suddenly we smelled dinner burning. I rushed into the kitchen to salvage it. Granted, it was only tomato soup, but she didn't want to throw away any food because she only had so much money.

I brought it to the couch, and she slurped and talked at the same time.

She started by admitting that confessing to me was the only way she knew to save her soul. With no regard for my feelings, she continued the story of how I came into the world.

My mom was already a single mother at the time. She had tried to abort me, taking pills that "were guaranteed to work." All she did was spot a little.

Abortions were not legal back then. In desperation, her only option was to get a back-alley abortion, since she was neither wealthy nor able to get to New York where you could get a real doctor. She had a friend who knew a person who knew a person who performed abortions at his house. Mom borrowed $200 from her mother and brought it with her that awful night in early May, forty-three years ago.

She tentatively knocked at the door of the appointed location. A toothless lady opened the door with the chain lock remaining in place. Mom woodenly spoke the words she'd been given as the code: "I want to buy a dog."

The lady let Mom in and told her to wait on a kitchen chair in the middle of a ratty living room. The floor was stained and smelled like piss. There were garbage bags covering the windows. Mom wondered if this was because of the cold Chicago weather or to keep people from looking in to this place of death. She probably should have run, she thought, but she was desperate.

Soon the lady led Mom into the kitchen. She had to take off her skirt and get on the kitchen table, which was up on blocks, the lower half higher than the top.

A man approached. He looked dirty, and without a word of hello to calm her, he asked how far along she was. Mom said she figured she was around four months. The man asked if she wanted to get rid of it. Mom just nodded. He asked if she was a whore and if she got knocked up from a one-night stand. Mom explained she was poor and was unable to afford another child since she had a son already. An adored son.

The room smelled of dirty laundry, blood, newspapers, and rubbing alcohol. Mom said she wished she'd taken a Seconal or had a drink before coming to this dirty, dingy room.

He started the procedure. Yellowed teeth and unshaven face hovering between her legs. Vivid images burned in her mind, connected to shame, pain, and fear.

Mom paused here to finish her soup before continuing the story.

Although the man had already started the procedure, my mother thought about leaving when he said, "This is going to hurt, but don't move or scream out."

She shivered, telling me it was the most agony she'd ever experienced in her life. She was twenty years old, and even though she had given birth to a boy three and a half years earlier, this was like nothing she had ever gone through. Stabbing pain and cramps.

The man followed the procedure with a few terse words, saying, "You'll bleed for a few days and then it will be gone."

Mom left through the back door.

There was a girl lying outside with a pool of blood beneath her—unconscious or dead, Mom couldn't tell. She banged on the back door.

"Please help me! There's a dead girl out here!"

The toothless woman came out and took in the scene. "Help me move her to the street where there's a pay phone," she said.

Mom and the lady lifted the girl. Mom checked her pulse. It was faint but still there. They hauled this barely alive body to the street corner.

The woman said menacingly, "Remember you were never here, and neither was she. You don't want nothin' happening to that little son of yours." Then she disappeared.

Mom looked for the pay phone. It was up half a block. She searched her purse for a dime to call an ambulance. As soon as she'd made the call, she left. She had terrible cramps and soon was barely able to walk. She made it home block by block, leaving a blood trail behind.

When she arrived home, Mom took a couple of aspirins and a Seconal and went to bed, telling Nanny (her mother) that she had a bad period and cramps. This was not unusual, so Nanny didn't ask any more questions.

When Mom woke up the next day, she glanced around her room, all groggy, seeing bright sun shining in through the curtains, made from cheap sheets. Her mattress was one found beside the road, lumpy and smelling of mold. Mom said she lay in the fetal position for a while before getting up and acting like it was a normal day.

A few days later Mom stopped bleeding. She told me she tried to give herself several bleach douches to prevent infection. I can't even imagine the smell and the raw pain from bleaching your private parts. Mom admitted she drank and took Seconal for the next two months.

*   *   *

On July 6, 1962, two months later, Mom got a terrible backache and cramps. It got so bad that she decided to go to the hospital. She called a cab. Nearing the hospital, she felt pressure like she was going to have a bowel movement. She thought, "Great—I'm going to the hospital for constipation." Just then she began to scream.

The cab driver pulled up in front of Cook County Hospital and said, "Lady, you're crazy. Get out of this cab!" He didn't even wait for her to pay. Which was just as well, as she had no money.

She almost got to the door when she had to lie down. A nurse rushed out to see what was wrong. Mom let out a guttural scream and out I came.

Turns out she'd been six months pregnant.

I gave a weak cry; my mom fainted.

They rushed me to the preemie unit. I had to be taken to a separate nursery because I was so little and considered an "unsterile birth." I weighed one pound, twelve ounces.

Mom checked herself out against medical advice later that same day—to go to work—starting a pattern that would shroud the rest of our life together.

*   *   *

Mom named me Emory after a doll she had as a child.

I stayed in the hospital for almost four months. Preemie babies couldn't come home until they were four pounds. Mom never came to visit. The hospital had to call her when it was time for me to come home.

She waited until after work to pick me up. The nurses tried to explain how to take care of my special needs. Mom responded, "I already have one kid at home. I know how to do this." She then called a cab, laid me on the seat, and we went to our first home on the South Side of Chicago.

Mom had no money and was not able to provide for the basic needs of a newborn, let alone a premature baby. I slept in a dresser drawer. Mom put me across the room from her so she didn't have to hear me cry at night. I was supposed to be fed every two hours, but because she had to work, Mom couldn't be awakened at night.

Thus began our long non-bonding experience.

I left my mother's house that day without being able to confess my own secret—that I loved a woman. She wouldn't have cared, anyway. Her confession was, indeed, what I had needed to know, but it had all been for her—her own pathetic attempt to save her soul from hell. None of it had been to really see me—to recognize that I had my own story to tell.

CHAPTER 2

Pictures

When I arrived home from visiting Mom I pulled out the old scrapbook my grandma had made for me. One tattered snapshot showed a three-and-a-half-year-old Ronny leaning over the dresser drawer, feeding and taking care of me.

I looked at another picture of my mom with her arm around Ronny as he held me. She wasn't touching me. I looked like a raw chicken with translucent skin and thin fingernails. I looked like this for nearly ten months. When people saw me, they just said, "What a tiny baby," not "What a cute baby." I was only three pounds when this photo was taken. I had lost weight since I wasn't being fed every two hours as the nurses had directed.

This was the beginning of Ronny being the "man of the house," a title he was not ready to assume and probably resented. Yet my brave brother stepped up and took on the care of a premature baby. I know he is solely responsible for my surviving my first year on this Earth.

*   *   *

Mom worked every day and left Ronny in charge of me. She had Nanny there just in case. Nanny worked nights and slept in the far bedroom. She didn't want to hear us. She needed her sleep so she could work. Ronny was the only parent I had. I'm sure he wanted to be playing with his friends, but he had to be there to protect me, as there was no one else to do so.

It was a heavy burden to bear. Ronny had to make sandwiches, clean, and take care of me because Mom was never home. When she wasn't working, she was in some bar. She used prescription pills, snorted coke, and smoked marijuana to come down from the coke. She smelled of smoke and alcohol, and not even a shower would get it off her skin. It was in her pores. My mom brought home many men who smelled of beer and cheap aftershave. She was in search of a husband and a father for these two kids.

There is a picture of me on my first birthday in a dress and a bonnet, looking stunned. Those were the days when cameras had flash cubes on top. They made a big flash and your eyes always looked demon red in the center. I was tied in a chair at the waist and chest since I was barely able to sit. They put me in that chair on top of two Chicago phonebooks, for height. The picture showed a white cake with cherries on top. It was a rum cake, not the kind children usually like, or eat.

Another picture showed my brother and me playing on the living-room floor with a large old TV in the background. I remember the rabbit ears on top, wrapped in tinfoil. I was almost three.

This photo brought an odd memory to mind. One day when my mom was gone that old television blew a tube, hurling black smoke throughout the apartment. Six-year-old Ronny took me outside to the hall and then went back into the kitchen and called the fire department. I was scared and hoped Ronny would return soon. When he came back for me his face was pale and smudged with smoke. That was the first time I'd ever seen him even mildly frightened.

We sat on the steps on the landing. The downstairs neighbor, Silvia, had smelled smoke and opened the door to see us sitting on the landing. She invited us into her apartment to wait for the firefighters and our mother. Her place smelled like sausage. That was the most vivid memory I had about living there: All the apartments were a melting pot of food. Polish, Lithuanian, Chinese, etc.

＊　　　　＊　　　　＊

I was rarely out in public during those years, so I didn't have the chance to develop many social skills. Once, Ronny and I and Mom and Mom's new boyfriend went to a nice restaurant called the Stockyard Inn. It was by the Chicago stockyards, famous for being the place where livestock were brought in on trains and butchered. I lost my appetite because of the awful smell outside.

My mom and her boyfriend ordered steak and martinis. Mom was appalled when I ordered a six-dollar peanut butter and jelly sandwich. I thought at a fancy restaurant they would have a good peanut butter and jelly sandwich, but the bread was stale and the sandwich had only one triangle piece with some green parsley next to it. Mom was mad for the rest of the night.

I laugh now. What a typical young-kid move. Now restaurants usually have a separate kids' menu. I was ahead of the times on that one.

＊　　　　＊　　　　＊

Our family lived in a courtyard-like place with four buildings surrounding a big cement area where the kids played. It was a square with no exit except through people's apartments.

One day I stuck my new shoe into a drain hole in the courtyard. I pulled and pulled until my foot came out of the shoe, which remained firmly stuck. I cried because I had just gotten them that week. They were Red Ball Jets. I knew Mom would kill me, as they cost two dollars—the same as two gallons of milk.

"Ronny, my shoe is stuck," I called out. I always depended on him for things like this. I showed him the little red shoe. He fished his arm down the drain hole and grabbed the shoe and tried to pry it out. He lay down on the cement for a better reach.

Plop! the shoe said as it came out.

Ronny said nothing—just leaned down and put the shoe back on my tiny foot and tied it tight. Then he returned to his friends who were bouncing a ball against the wall.

I watched him in awe. He was the bravest and strongest person I'd ever met.

Soon he came and took me by the hand and led me upstairs. I sat on the floor playing with blocks as he took the SpaghettiOs and put them in a pot on the stove. He used his little stool to climb up to the stove. I lapped up the SpaghettiOs and ended up having the telltale mustache, compliments of Campbell's.

Ronny was seven and I was three and a half.

CHAPTER 3

Sent Away

When I was four, Mom sent me away to Dwight, Illinois, a small town about seventy miles south of Chicago. She kept Ronny with her in Chicago.

She sent me to live with a friend who worked with Mickey, her boyfriend at the time. Bernie and Brad had five boys and had always wanted a girl. At first, they treated me well. But after a few months the boys began to play terrible jokes on me. Like giving me chocolate, which I loved. It turned out to be Ex-Lax. At that age I didn't know what diarrhea was, so when Bernie gave me a bath, I pooped all over the tub.

Bernie was livid. "As punishment, you will take a cold shower to get all the poop off the tub."

I had to wipe everything down with a funny-smelling spray, climbing into the bathtub to reach all the spots. As I was getting out, I fell and hit my head on the tub. When I saw the blood, I began to scream. Bernie came in, eyes blazing. She grabbed me and said, "Now you have to clean up the blood after the bleeding stops."

Unfortunately, the bleeding did not stop. The wound opened, and I could see white underneath. I went to Bernie, careful to hold the washcloth on my head so I would not bleed everywhere along the way. Bernie said, "Damn—now we have to go to the doctor."

Outside the doctor's office I became scared again and began to cry silent tears. Bernie grasped my hand hard and pinched my shoulder. "You better be good, or you'll get a spanking when you get home."

When she opened the door to the office, I heard a bell. I looked up on the door and saw it; it was pretty and gold.

The office smelled of antiseptic. I sat on a hard plastic chair. The colors were muted, darker than what you would find in a waiting room today.

As we sat down, I kept watching the bell and swinging my legs.

Soon my name was called by a pretty nurse with long blonde hair and blue eyes. She led us to a small room.

"Are you all set?" she asked, smiling. "The doctor will see you shortly."

She left the room and shut the door. I could hear a baby crying and it made me feel queasy.

Soon the doctor came in. He was wearing a white starched coat and one of those headbands with a mirror on it. He looked at me. "I bet I can guess why you are here," he said with a gentle voice. "Let's see that sore on your head. Oh, it looks like you'll need stitches."

I started to worry because I didn't know what that word meant. I figured it was bad.

The nurse came back and said, "Okay, ready, sweetie?" She started putting things on a table—I was too small to see—and then covered everything with paper. She put me in a chair that went up and down and leaned me back. The nurse had a brown bottle containing a brownish-red liquid she put on the cut. She put a paper over my eyes to protect them and started pouring the medicine on my head. It was cold, so I started to sniffle.

The doctor came in and moved toward the table. I saw the needle in his hand as he uncovered the wound. He moved the needle closer to my head and I felt a sting like the bee that I'd stepped on the previous summer. I screamed loudly.

Bernie covered my mouth with a washcloth. I gagged and nearly threw up.

After a few moments, the doctor left. Soon after the nurse with the blonde hair came in and touched my head. I was surprised the wound didn't hurt.

The doctor came back and said, "Now this won't hurt at all. I used that other needle to give you a shot, so your cut wouldn't hurt anymore."

11

I doubted that, but stopped screaming. He touched my head and poked around a bit. I could feel him touching me, but it didn't hurt. Then I felt something move across my face.

"I feel a spiderweb on my face!" I yelled, and tried to swat it away.

The nurse said, "Don't worry, sweetie—that's just the doctor. He's using that thread to fix your cut. He'll be done soon and then I'll give you a sucker."

I liked suckers and decided to just be still and wait.

Soon the doctor was all done. I sat there awaiting my prize as they took the towel off my head.

We left the office, with me happily licking the sucker. I didn't get a spanking, so I must have been good.

*   *   *

My mom came the next day. I overheard her talking with Bernie.

Mom said, "Bernie, I want her home. Also, she now has stitches in her head—obviously she wasn't being watched."

"I thought you were going to leave her here for at least a few years," Bernie said. "And that fall was an accident."

Mom was stern when she said, "She is my daughter and I want her back. Thank you for taking care of her, but I need you to pack her clothes." My mom was making her mad face.

Bernie looked sad. Her eyes got all watery and her lip trembled.

I wanted to give her a hug but didn't want them to know I'd been listening. I was happy to hear that my mom wanted me.

I learned later that my mother never went back to get my things. Bernie kept them, just in case my mom changed her mind.

I rode home in the back, with the window open. My mom was smoking, with the little triangle window open. She also played the CB real loud.

"Mom, I have to throw up," I said. I started choking on the vomit I was trying to hold in.

"Don't puke in the car! Let me pull over." She seemed distressed. She got to the side of the road just as I was climbing out of the backseat. I projectile-vomited all over the grass.

"We made it," she said, relieved.

CHAPTER 4

Nursery School

When I got back to Chicago, I went to nursery school. There were blocks to play with and coloring to do, two of my favorite things. I was happy there.

"Teacher, would you be my mommy?" I was an anxious child, always on alert. That's how I felt, even at age four.

The teacher replied, "No, I can't be your mommy. You already have a mommy."

"But not a good one like you."

She just smiled, the corners of her eyes watery. "Let's go get the blocks. I know you like all of the colors."

One afternoon I saw my mom in the classroom doorway. She had on a brown dress. I didn't really like it because it had polka dots on it. I didn't like polka dots even though they looked nice with my mother's frosted brown hair.

Mom looked angry. I guess the teacher had called her and told her I'd thrown up on my mat and my clothes. Now she'd have to find someone to watch me for the afternoon, or at least for three hours.

I heard her ask, "Where's my daughter?"

The teacher said, "She's in another section by herself so she wouldn't get the other children sick."

I remember feeling lonely lying there, staring at the ceiling, away from the toys and my friends.

My mom picked me up and then put me back down, saying, "Oh, you smell like puke." She stripped me in the street and put my clothes in the trunk. Then she put me in the car in my underwear. I was so embarrassed. My mom had borrowed our neighbor Mr. Bacon's big blue car. He lived downstairs.

Mother, can you hear me now?

Mom called Nanny, who wasn't working that day, to take care of me until Ronny got home. Mom had moved out of her mother's house. Nanny was nice to me, but she thought my mom should take care of her own issues.

Mom was still drinking and leaving us alone. Back then no one reported this kind of thing. It was common to leave your kids at home alone. It was well known that you never called Family Services. Some people hit their children so hard they had bruises. But no one cared enough to mess in other people's business.

*   *   *

Mom came home one Friday and told Ronny and me, "Uncle George died in Kentucky, where Great-Grandma Annie Moore lives."

"Who's Uncle George?" I asked, because I'd never heard of him.

"Uncle George was Great-Grandma Annie's brother."

I wanted to be sad, but I didn't even know who he was. I was four and a half years old.

We left for Kentucky the next day, in Mr. Bacon's car. It seemed like a long way to drive. It was fun looking out the windows at the farms with their red tractors and cows. Some farms even had horses. I had never seen these things. In Kentucky they had a lot of bluish grass along the road. In Illinois the grass was green.

We went to the house of a lady I didn't know, with a lot of people and a lot of food.

I had never had pickles before. These came in a clear glass jar with a top that needed a bottle opener. It opened with a pop. I realize now they were pickles that she grew in her garden and canned. I'd like some right now.

"Would you like to try these pickles?" Aunt Minee asked.

I licked it.

"I think it's spoiled," I said, and gave it to my aunt Evelyn so I didn't hurt Aunt Minee's feelings.

15

I was led into the dining room where there was a dead man on the table. Mom lifted me up to see him. I guessed this was Uncle George. His face was the color of the paste I had at home. She set me back on the floor.

"How did he die?" I asked quietly.

Mom said, "It was his heart. It was broken, and they didn't have enough money to get it fixed at the big hospital."

I wondered if my heart would break. If I ran real fast it would hit my chest, hard.

"Did Uncle George break his heart from running too fast?" I asked.

"No," Mom said. "Hush now."

I went back to the kitchen and saw shiny dishes on the wall. One looked like a fish and the other like a round cake with bumps. There was even one on the table with Jell-O in it. Great-Grandma Annie came to the table and turned the bowl of Jell-O upside down on a plate. It wiggled but stayed in the same shape as the bowl.

My mom said it was called a Jell-O mold. "Would you like some?"

I liked Jell-O but not mold, so I said, "No, thank you."

I looked at all the food. I was hungry, but not for anything I saw on the table.

Soon Ronny came over with a plate for me. It had applesauce, mac and cheese, a hot dog with ketchup, and a big brownie as big as my hand. I wished Ronny had brought me one as big as his hand. I licked off all the frosting and then ate the brownie.

After I'd eaten the other things, Ronny took me to the bathroom to clean up. "You have an orange mustache from the Hi-C," he said.

I was grateful that the bathroom was in the house, as many homes in the area did not have indoor plumbing. The bathroom was decorated with homemade curtains; they were blue, with polka dots. I liked the polka dots on those curtains despite hating my mom's dress. I guess she liked it. It was form-fitting and showed off her great figure.

"You know, Sis, I will always take care of you," Ronny said when I came out of the bathroom. He hugged me and led me outside where there were lots of kids, called cousins. We played in the dust and rocks.

I looked up the hill and saw some boys with Ronny; they were sliding down the hill on their butts, and with a sled. In Chicago we had sleds, but we only used them in the snow. We'd never had one of our own but some neighbors did, and they let me sit on it as they pulled me all around the snowy concrete. It made a screeching noise on the concrete.

CHAPTER 5

Kentucky

Kentucky was way more fun than Chicago. The cousins showed us their cows and chickens. They had a horse called "Mule."

After we'd played with them for a while, Mom came out and said, "Time to go."

But we didn't go home. Mom drove just a bit and then turned off the main road and drove over a bridge made of wood, just big enough for the car to fit. We came to the end of the road where there was a little creek. Mom drove Mr. Bacon's blue car right through it.

"Roll up your windows," she said.

I said, "I like looking at the water. I don't want to roll up the window."

Mom said, "Just do it."

The trees scratched the windows. It scared me. There wasn't very much water, but I wondered where we were going. I thought Mom was drunk-driving as she drove through the creek and up a little hill where the creek turned the other way.

We came to a house that she said was Great-Grandma Annie's. We walked past this little house that had only three sides. There were black dusty rocks all around.

"What are those black rocks?" I asked.

"Coal," Mom said.

Then we passed a pile of logs. I wondered what they were for.

We went up Great-Grandma Annie Moore's steps and I saw more wood under a plastic tarp. There were a few logs on the porch, and some rocking chairs.

"Can I sit on the chairs, Mom?"

A quick "No" was all she said.

Ronny told me to look, and I saw a snake. A real snake that was an orange color. Ronny called it a copperhead.

"Can I play with the snake?"

Ronny said, "They can kill you dead."

I didn't want to be like Uncle George on the dining-room table, so I thought I'd better stay away.

We went inside and sat on a couch. There was a velvet picture of a man sitting at the middle of the table with many men alongside him.

"Who are they? Are they relatives?"

"No," Mom said. "It's Jesus with his disciples."

I had heard briefly about him. He was the Virgin Mary's son. We prayed to him but also to the Virgin Mary and the saints. There were lots of saints. I couldn't keep them straight.

I had never seen this many men with long hair before. Across from the picture of Jesus there was a fireplace. Mom brought in some wood from the porch and put it in the fireplace. Soon I saw a fire in the living room!

"There's a fire in the house—we need to get out!" I was so sheltered I'd never seen an indoor fireplace before.

Ronny said, "This fire is okay, as long as it stays in the fireplace."

Ronny kept moving the wood in the fire around with a poker. There was a little broom and pan on a holder by the fireplace. We watched the fire for a little bit and then Mom said, "Time for bed, kids."

At the same time, we both said, "We don't want to go to bed."

Ronny called "Jinx," which meant I owed him a Coke. It didn't matter to me because we never had Coke anyway, except at a Woolworth's counter once. I remembered I had French fries. I could almost taste them, they were so good.

On the way to bed, I looked over at the kitchen and saw there were pies on the windowsill.

"Mom, can I taste the pie?"

Mom firmly said, "No."

"Why not?" I whined.

"Because they are Great-Grandma Annie's, not ours."

"I'm sure she wouldn't mind. She is our great-grandma."

I really wanted to taste those pies. They looked like cherry and apple, my favorites. I also loved chocolate, but you didn't see much of that around here. They did have rhubarb and mincemeat, which I thought was gross.

Mom just grabbed my hand and led me to the bedroom. Ronny walked behind us. It felt a little cold after the warmth of the fire.

The bed had ropes underneath to hold up the feather mattress. The pillows had feathers too. The feathers could come through the pillowcase and poke you lightly in the cheek, but I didn't mind because I sank in so nicely. Mom covered us with a checkered blanket that looked like a star inside a circle. It was very warm and beautiful. Mom said it was a quilt that Great-Grandma Annie made. I attempted to make quilts later in life, but they quickly turned into table runners. I couldn't handle the large size.

"You may both sleep in your clothes to keep you warm."

I woke up in the morning to a funny sound like a screaming bird, but I thought it said a kind of word: Cock-a-doodle-doo.

Mom was gone, and Great-Grandma Annie was there sleeping in the next bed.

*   *   *

Great-Grandma Annie got us up, saying, "Time for chores."

Ronny moaned. I didn't know why he was upset.

We went outside to gather eggs. "Don't forget to watch for snakes," Grandma said. She explained that sometimes there were snakes in the chicken coop, stealing eggs.

"What do we do if we find one?" I asked.

"Stay away from them. They're dangerous," said Grandma.

We went outside to the coop and found the chickens. They were sitting in rows on both sides, perched on sticks. Ronny said, "Watch this." He stuck his hand under the chicken and brought his arm out and there was an egg! He reached in again and then another time for a total of three eggs. He went down both rows and ended up holding a full basket, which he carefully brought inside.

Next we went back to feed the chickens. We sprinkled seeds on the ground and they used their beaks to peck at the food. Ronny took me around the back of the coop where I saw little balls of fluffy yellow baby chicks.

When we were almost done, I said, "Listen—I hear a baby's rattle. Let's look for the baby."

Ronny grabbed me by the hand and said, "Run! It's a rattlesnake!"

"I want to see it!" The last snake we'd seen didn't have a rattle. I wanted to see where the rattle was coming from.

My brother pulled me along and dragged me up the porch steps.

"Stand here, and you can see the snake."

Soon enough, a big snake with diamonds and a rattle on the end appeared. The chickens ran away but I could see that the snake had grabbed one of the fluffy yellow babies.

I grabbed my brother's hand, saying, "Let's go! We have to save the baby chick from that mean snake!"

My brother pulled me back up the steps and took me inside and told Great-Grandma Annie what had happened.

*   *   *

Later that day Great-Grandma Annie said, "Time to take a bath."

I said, "I have to go poopy first."

Grandma helped me take my pants off and led me outside down the path by the vegetable garden to this awful-smelling little shed. She opened the door. There were two holes on top of a raised wooden shelf. She looked down the hole for snakes. I looked down there and saw piles of poop.

"I'm not going to go poopy here. Other people's poop might get on me, or I might fall in and snakes will eat me."

Grandma held me up so I wouldn't fall in. I screamed, and then she took me back to the house. She told me to "poop in the grass in the backyard." From then on, that's where I pooped. There was a house called the smokehouse back there, too. I was amazed there was a house just to smoke in. My mom smoked in our house; there was no special building for it.

Then it was time for the promised bath. My grandma went to a pipe in the creek where water came out. The water was cold, and Grandma had to put it on the stove to heat it up. She brought out a big tub and poured in the hot water.

I put my hand on my hip and said, "You want me to take a bath in a tub in the kitchen. Someone might come in and see me." Grandma assured me no one was coming in. When the water had cooled a little, she put me in the tub. She washed me with some scratchy soap. Then she went to cook lunch.

I wanted a drink of water, but I couldn't find a faucet. Grandma led me to a big bucket with something called a dipper. We all drank out of the same bucket. I was afraid I would get cooties.

*   *   *

My brother went to school in Kentucky, but I didn't. This was before kindergarten was mandatory.

One morning I followed my brother as far as the creek on his walk to school. I came back into the yard and saw the big snake with the rattle on it. My grandma came out just in time to see me grab for the snake.

"Get away from there and come inside!" she yelled.

I went and sat on one of the porch chairs and pouted. I thought it would be fun to have a pet snake. Suddenly I heard singing up the holler. That's what they called the road and the woods. The singing got louder.

I went into the house and said, "There is someone singing up the holler."

Grandma said, "That's your uncle Luther."

I laughed at the name.

I went out to see my uncle emerge from the hills. He was the tallest person I'd ever seen, and you know what? He had a wooden leg! You could knock on it just like a wooden table. I noticed he was carrying two buckets of water.

"Why is he carrying two buckets of water? He must be very thirsty."

Grandma said, "It's from his well. Mine is broken." She pointed out a place where there were boards piled high. She said, "Never stand on those boards or you'll fall down the well." I supposed the well was a giant hole leading to the center of the Earth, where the Devil lived.

My uncle could whistle through his teeth. He also could spit a long way, and he taught me how to do it. My spit was clear and I couldn't spit very far. His was brown, because he was always chewing something that made his lower lip push out. I thought it was a special kind of bubblegum, but he wouldn't let me have any. He said it was like smoking, which he'd started doing at age nine. I could hardly wait to be nine so I could smoke and chew the brown gum.

I never chewed or smoked in my adult life.

CHAPTER 6

Catholic School

We left Kentucky when I was almost five. I had to start school in Chicago. We went to a Catholic school nearby called Assumption.

I came home after three days and said, "I've decided to be a nun. I love their long black dresses, and they have no hair. They keep their hands in enormous pockets."

I loved the smell of crayons but not the taste. I tried several colors but they all tasted the same. I also liked the taste of paste. There was a little brush in the jar and I tried to brush my teeth with it, but it didn't work out as planned. It seems I was a weird child and not well liked. Perhaps it was the choppy haircut my mom gave me or my dirty uniform. The nuns often talked to my mom about my hygiene, and about washing my uniform.

Mom came to the school and yelled at Sister Mary Kevin.

"I'm not like those rich bitches here who can afford nice things. I work for a living, and her brother gets her ready and does the laundry. So, don't blame me if things aren't perfect. I pay a lot of money for her to go to this school and I don't want to be harassed."

Oh no, I thought. She yelled at a nun! I think you go to hell for that.

Sister Mary Kevin said, "Okay, we will work it out."

One day I found a loose screw hanging underneath my desk. I tried to take it off but it made a squeaking noise. I liked the noise.

"Who's making that noise?" Sister Mary Kevin asked.

I raised my hand and every good Catholic kid pointed to me. For this misdemeanor I had to stand with my nose pressed to a circle on the board. I had to stand on my tippy toes. To this day, I hate the smell of chalk.

Misery loves company, and I felt better after another girl kept slipping her shoe off. The nun took her shoe and threw it outside. I felt bad for her because our plaid uniforms and special shoes cost a lot of money. We all wore the same thing: white shirts with Peter Pan collars, plaid jumpers, maroon tights, and maroon shoes. I knew that girl did not have a lot of money. Her skin was light brown and she had the nicest friendly smile and cute ponytails on each side of her head. I was so jealous. I had short hair my mom curled with a Toni's home perm. I didn't know who Toni was, but she made my hair harder to brush. Before we went to second Mass and lunch, Sister gave the nice girl her shoe back. It was on the windowsill the whole time. I thought it was mean to tease the poor girl. She cried all morning; I could hear her sniffles.

At recess we played a game called Red Rover. There were two equal teams. They would hold hands and say, "Red Rover, Red Rover, send (insert child's name here) right over." The person who was called would run as fast as he or she could and try to break between the tightly clasped hands. I was always called last. I could never figure out why. I was called last for every game they played. It hurt my feelings and made me sad.

Soon the bell would ring. You had to freeze in place until the second bell rang. Then you ran to get in line to go back into school. The recess nun would stand there and mark off names when you passed through the line. I wondered if they did this to make sure no one escaped or was kidnapped.

I got hit with a ruler a lot. I have scars to prove it. They wanted me to write with my right hand. They also wanted me to lose the backhand style some left-handers use to write.

Before the day started, we went to Mass. The priest spoke in Latin. I couldn't understand a word. So, what did I do? I turned around and waved to Sister Mary Kevin. When we got to class, I had to stand in the smelly coat room. Eddie's coat smelled the worst—like wet puppies.

You know what's gross? (Those with weak stomachs, skip this paragraph.) Boogers. A kid named Tommy ate his boogers. Not just the dry ones he just picked from his nose but the wet, long, stringy ones too. I may have been a paste and crayon eater, but I was no booger eater. (Okay, I warned you.)

We lived only a few blocks from the school, on Damen Avenue, across from the park where my brother taught me to ride a bike. Down the street from the taco place. The tacos were so good we ate them a lot for lunch. Our block always smelled like those yummy tacos.

It was a great week when we were off from school for a few days. Sometimes Nanny would cook extra food so all Ronny had to do was heat it up in a pan. We'd have TV dinners one day and hotdogs the next. We would have carrot sticks as a snack, and lunch was PB&J. Breakfast the next day was Spam and eggs.

CHAPTER 7

The Move

We moved to a bigger place on 38th Street when I was five. My brother walked me to Davis School every day because I was still young. Ronny spent his recess throwing a ball against the wall with everyone trying to catch it. If they caught it with no bouncing it was 500 points; each bounce brought down the score by 100. Ronny was very good at this game, as he was low to the ground and very fast. He caught all the balls except the very high ones.

My sister Rachael was born in our new apartment. I didn't even know my mom was pregnant, so I was surprised when she arrived. I wanted to play with this doll-like baby all the time. I even tried to get in her crib.

Rachael spent the day in a playpen. I always played quietly with my toys nearby; at least I thought I was quiet. The adults around me didn't agree. Ronny still watched me when mom was at work. All Rachael did was poop and puke but she was still cute. She needed a lot of time from my mom and Nanny. Rachael spent the days at Nanny's house. When I was around, my mom would just say things like "When Tooter comes into the room, even the pictures fall off the wall." She never called me by my real name until years later. I thought the nickname was rude. It was given to me as a baby because I farted all the time.

I didn't know this at the time, but my new sister was my second dad's child. My brother and I shared the same dad, John. My sister was my "middle" dad's, Stan. Following the same routine as before, now Ronny watched over both of us.

By the time I was five my mother had a new boyfriend named Bill. He wanted to get to know us, and tried several things to get us to like him. He took us to Riverview Amusement Park where I went on all the rides for little kids. It was the greatest! He took us to Santa's Village. You could go there even though it wasn't Christmas. It was so fun. I did start to like my possible new dad.

My mom and Bill Brown got married after my sister Rachael was born. My mom wore a blue dress and my new dad wore a navy suit. Nanny stood with her and a man named Jim Champion stood with my new dad.

One day I was outside in the alley. Pay dirt! I found a refrigerator box. I pulled it into the yard after hitting at the rats. I wasn't afraid of them when I was a kid, but now I'm terrified of them and their smaller counterparts, mice.

I was happily playing with the big box, crawling through it and standing it up, but I was too short to climb in. Mom came out and said "Get away from that dirty old box." I couldn't resist playing with it. Mom came out again and said, "Now you will pay for not listening to me." She stuffed me in the box and taped the top and bottom with packing tape.

I was afraid. The box was taped and I was trapped. I started to panic. I started hitting and punching the box, to no avail. I pushed hard until I'd turned the box over. I was able to kick through the side and crawled out of the little opening.

My mom came back out and saw me out of the box. "I told you to stay in there!" she yelled. She pulled down my pants and started spanking me. I was screaming and crying, as she was using a belt. The belt stung on my bare bottom and I started to run away from it. She held me with one hand and whipped me with the other. I kept twisting and the belt wrapped around my legs. She just kept going and I kept screaming. I was afraid she would never quit.

Soon, my stepdad Bill came out and said, "Elise, stop— she's had enough. Come in the house." He came over and looked at the bruises already forming on my bottom. He took me inside and gave me an ice pack to sit on. It made my bottom very cold, and as it melted, it felt like I'd peed all over myself. He sent me to my room—not as a punishment, but to keep me out of Mom's way.

*   *   *

It was the sixties, early seventies, and there were race riots going on all around us in Chicago. Our apartment was getting more expensive. My mom took us to look for another apartment in the Near North Side, and we saw the housing projects known as Cabrini-Green. Mom said they used to be called war homes, and then later they became housing projects for the poor. She said there were others like these called the Robert Taylor homes. These were located on State Street, on the South Side.

We went a long way down State Street. You could see pretty storefronts like Macy's at Christmastime. Mom said we might have to live at the Robert Taylor homes or Cabrini-Green if we continued to be "bad kids."

After seeing both places, I knew I didn't want to live at either one. I wanted our own separate apartment. The only thing was, the apartments next to us were so close you could stand between them, put your hands on both walls, and climb up. I was caught doing this on more than one occasion. My punishment: The Belt.

*   *   *

One night my mom drove Ronny and me to a bar. We stayed in the car in the parking lot. My brother told me the sign nearby said "Federal Drive." It was noisy and there was a lot of litter everywhere. I saw my mom come out. She didn't come to our car; she went into a hotel. A man followed her out and gave her money and a card. (Maybe a phone number?) She stuffed the money in her bra and walked into a bar that said "Go Go Girls."

When she came out the next time, she had another man with her, and they went to the same hotel. I started to fall asleep in the car. The last thing I remember was some girls coming out of the go-go bar. They had tall white boots, long hair, and very short dresses, and wore lots of makeup. I hoped I could get a pair of boots like that someday. They looked so cool.

We slept in the car the whole night. I was scared because it was dark and there were strangers all around the area. Mom came back to the car when the sun was shining.

"You kids be quiet now; I have to sleep. Here, eat these."

She pulled some cheese crackers out of her purse, along with some pills she instructed us to take.

I choked twice trying to take them before my mom said, "Wash it down with this coffee." The coffee was warm but I got the pill down.

We ate in silence. Soon my mother was asleep. I knew it because she was grinding her teeth and snoring. I hated the sound of that grinding.

Soon I had to pee. Ronny quietly opened the door and took me to a gas station nearby. I was afraid Mom would wake up and leave us and we would have to go to the bad kids' homes. I felt like we were lost but luckily Ronny remembered where we were. Somehow, he always did.

We did this for three days. I guessed this was our new home. I wasn't afraid because I knew Ronny would take care of me.

When our mom left the car one night, my brother and I knocked on the back door of a restaurant. The man who opened it just looked at us. My brave brother asked for some of the food they were going to throw away. The guy gave us a garbage bag of stuff to go to the dumpster. I found chicken and bread in there and that's what we ate that night. We ate hungrily with our hands and then wiped our hands on our pants.

After a few days we returned home just in time to see our stepdad Bill coming back after a week on the road, driving his truck. I ran to my bedroom and my bed and toys were still there! Soon there was a knock on my door and I heard Nanny talking. She brought my new sister Rachael in and laid her in the crib and told me to be quiet, as Rachael was sleeping.

CHAPTER 8

White Flight

Our neighborhood became unstable and my parents soon joined the "white flight" migration, moving to Dwight, where I'd lived for a while when I was four. My parents both worked in Chicago at the time, and stayed there even though they moved us kids seventy miles away. My mother worked at Holsum Bakery and later, in hotel management, while my stepdad worked as a truck driver for Navajo Freight. He was a union steward for the Teamsters, and each year would receive a bunch of steaks for Christmas. The only problem was when they had a strike. People started throwing bricks off the overpass at trucks who were caught not observing the strike.

"Dad, will people we know get killed?" I asked.

"Don't worry about such sad things," my dad said.

Five months later my youngest sister arrived. I was eight when she was born. This time I had noticed my mom getting fat.

My sister had curly red hair and green eyes. She was beautiful. I got to hold her when she got home. Her name was Roxy, short for Roxanne. I couldn't touch her head because she had soft spots. I wondered if she had soft spots on other places on her body. I worried that if I touched her too much she would get bruises. Yet somehow I couldn't resist touching her skin. It was soft like a feather. I had never felt anything so soft. She smelled good, too. I'd just follow her around and sniff her.

Initially my dad denied Roxy was his; Mom had been having an affair, so it wasn't too far-fetched that the baby wasn't his. When she was born my dad immediately knew

31

he was the father, as she looked just like him. Even so, my mom said to him, "It's not your baby, it's mine."

Roxy grew up to be "Daddy's little girl." Unlike Rachael, she was too young to go anywhere with me. Rachael followed me everywhere.

My aunt Belinda, Mom's sister, had a baby two months later. Aunt Bindy wasn't married, so I wondered how this could have happened. The baby was a cutie, with blue eyes and brown hair. She was named JoJo, short for Jolene Ann. Aunt Bindy worked as a switchboard operator at the Carlton Hotel and Mom managed the Carlton Inn in Chicago, while we kids stayed in Dwight with Great-Grandma Annie.

Before we moved I got to "help" Aunt Bindy work the switchboard. I put the plugs into the holes to connect people's calls. It was fun unless you accidentally disconnected someone. They would yell at Aunt Bindy and call her names. I thought it was unfair they were so mean to her. It was an accident, after all.

*   *   *

Great-Grandma Annie came to live with us in Dwight because a family member needed to live in her house in Kentucky. It was good for my mom as Grandma could watch us. Dwight had a population of 4,200 people at the time. They had a hospital for people with profound developmental disabilities. Before that it was a veterans hospital, and prior to this it was the famous Keeley Institute, known for the Keeley Cure for alcoholism. At four stories this building was the tallest in town. The two grocery stores both closed at eight p.m. Where did people get their food if they needed something at night?

In Chicago we opened fire hydrants when it was hot. This town didn't even have a pool, and no one used the fire hydrants except the firemen. In Dwight, most people had driveways to park in. Not so in Chicago. When it was cold, Chicago had a rule: If you dig out a parking space, you set a table in the space and no one else would use it. It was yours. In Chicago you had to pay for parking with a meter. Dwight had no meters, but every year you had to buy a village sticker.

In Dwight they have a big parade every year. People set their lawn chairs or blankets out the night before. There is an unwritten rule that you never take or move the lawn chairs. It probably looks strange to people passing through a town with all of these abandoned lawn chairs just sitting beside the road. You could walk freely in this town and everyone left their doors unlocked. You had to come in when the streetlights came on. If you called a wrong number you might spend twenty minutes talking with the person. If you stopped at the four-way stop, you could spend a few minutes there waving the other cars to go before you, because you knew they had to be at work earlier than you.

This small town had a lot of bars and churches. When my mom was in town, she spent most of the time at the bars and not the churches. She mostly left Dwight and went to a place a little way down the highway on Reed Road, so her car wouldn't be seen at all the bars in town. She knew every bar in town, but not her kids.

CHAPTER 9

A Man on the Moon

Around this time, I heard that a man had walked on the moon. They went there in a rocket. I thought that would be cool. We had a rocket in our park in Dwight, so I thought I would try that. I wondered if God was in the sky and maybe I'd meet him. I'd ask him to take all the alcohol away from my mother so we would have a normal family.

I went to the park and climbed to the second floor of the rocket. It was tall, and I'd never gone higher than this. It was scary. There was a slide on this level. I could have just gone down at this point, but no, I had a mission. I climbed to the next level and looked down. It was really high. I walked to the metal bars and looked all over the park. I tried to stick my head through the bars but thought better of that idea. I'd get my head stuck and then they would have to call the fire department.

I climbed all the way to the top. I found a beer bottle and a pink bra. Why would anyone leave a bra there? Then I saw half a bottle of beer. I decided to try it. I drank the whole thing. It didn't taste bad, but it made me dizzy. I decided I preferred pop over beer.

I walked over to the rocket's steering wheel and started to turn it, but it didn't move. After working at it for a few minutes, it finally budged. I started turning the wheel very fast and the rocket began to rock. This was great: I was going to the moon.

It never left the ground.

I decided to go home to call Neil Armstrong or Buzz Aldrin. What kind of name is Buzz, I wondered. Did his mom just look at her tiny baby and say, "Let's call him Buzz?" I wished I had a cool name like Buzz. I'd like to be called Rex, after the T-Rex. They were big, and everyone feared them.

I went home and asked my brother if he had Buzz the astronaut's number?

"Yes, I do. Why do you need it? Everyone knows his number. It's 1-312-865-123456789."

So, I called. I knew phone numbers were usually shorter. Ronny had given me a lot of numbers to dial. I hoped I wouldn't get in trouble; it might be long distance. We didn't call long distance unless it was for Mom, still working in Chicago.

I tentatively started dialing. It took a long time to dial a rotary phone because it had to go all the way around and come back before you could dial the next number. At Great-Grandma Annie's house in Kentucky, you could pick up the phone and hear other people talking. It was called a party line—although they never had a party, so I didn't know why they were always making plans on the phone.

I dialed the number. It took so long to make this call. Finally, the operator broke in and said, "What number are you trying to call?

"I want to call either Buzz or Neil, the astronauts."

"I can't give out those numbers, because they are unlisted."

"Can't you just direct me?" I asked. I knew something about operators, having worked with Aunt Bindy at the Carlton Hotel switchboard.

The operator said, "I don't have his number; I'm only a local operator." She said she would connect me to a long-distance operator.

I said, "No! Don't do that; I'll get in trouble."

She said since she would just be talking to another operator, it wouldn't be long distance.

"Okay, connect me," I said.

My brother was laughing this whole time. I told him to shut his quacker; I needed to hear.

The next operator came on and asked, "Whose number do you need?"

"I need to talk to Buzz the astronaut."

"Why do you need to talk to him?" she asked.

I told her the story about the rocket, and how I needed directions. She said, "Okay, I'll connect you."

I could hear her talking to a man on the phone, asking if he would talk to me. He said yes.

I asked if Buzz was his real name.

He said, "My birth name was Edwin Eugene, but my sister called me Buzz and it stuck."

"I want to be called Rex," I said.

"Okay, Rex, why did you call me?"

I explained my rocket situation.

He told me it had to be a real rocket.

"But there's a steering wheel and everything. You can climb all the way to the top."

He finally told me I couldn't fly that rocket. He said if I could make it to Florida, maybe I could see a rocket in person. I decided to start saving my allowance for a trip to Florida.

Then he asked me my address.

I said my mom wouldn't let me give my address to anyone, but he finally talked me into it. And what do you know, a week later, I got a package. My mom confiscated it at the door.

"Who would send you a package, little Tooter?" she said as she ripped it open.

A letter fell out, along with a cap, a book, a ring, and a cool necklace. I was so excited!

My mom looked at me and asked, "How did you get this stuff?"

I was scared. I said, "Ronny called."

"You're lying!" she screamed. She opened the garbage-can lid and tossed all my precious things in.

I ran to my bedroom and slammed the door.

Later on I tried to sneak the things out of the garbage can, but they were covered with coffee grounds and eggshells.

To this day I wonder if I spoke with Buzz or just a man who worked at NASA.

CHAPTER 10

The Park

One day I was babysitting my sister Rachael. She was three and I was eight. We had a breakfast of Quake cereal, and I gave her a Chocks vitamin. I packed us a lunch of peanut butter on Wonder bread and took her to the park, which was a block away.

It was nice to get away from my chores for a while. Grandma Annie had returned to Kentucky by this time, so as usual, it was Ronny taking care of me, Rachael, Roxy, and my cousin JoJo. JoJo had an absent father. My dad took over the role. JoJo had cerebral palsy and then my dad could insure her as Bindy had no insurance. The two little girls were just a few months old. I helped Ronny get bottles and diapers for the babies. You had to use diaper pins with the white cloth diapers—I stuck myself a lot trying to dress them—and then you had to soak the diapers when they were dirty. I had "potty duty," which meant soaking the diapers after they were washed out. You added bleach and put them in another pail before putting them into the washer. I used cold water and no bleach or detergent in the washer. When we got to the park I put Rachael in a baby swing while I sat in a big girl swing nearby. I swung higher and higher. I saw the shadow of my ponytail flying far out behind me. When I was going as high as I could, my little sister said, "Jump!" So I did. I even landed on my feet after flying so high. This "flying" was the only peace I had. It was like I was a floating angel.

Next, we sat on the ground and had our lunch. The grass was just long enough to tickle our feet. I tried to whistle through a piece of grass, thinking maybe this time I'd get a good piece of grass and the whistle would work. Nope.

"It's time to go home, Rachael," I told her.

She trudged behind me, and we crossed North Street without a problem. The next street was busy. It was a famous street called Old Route 66, where we lived. We were holding hands, waiting for a white van to pass so we could cross over to our house.

Rachael got spooked and let go of my hand. I heard the screeching of tires, and when I looked I saw my sister lying in the road.

I walked slowly over to her, and when she turned her head, I saw blood in her ear.

I hadn't seen much blood in my life, and I freaked.

Soon an ambulance appeared. It looked like one of those cars that take dead bodies to the funeral home. Not like my Uncle George's funeral, which was in a house, but a place where they take your blood out and put water in, so you don't rot.

"Where is your mother?" the men in the ambulance asked me.

"Check the bars," I said. "That's where she usually is when she's in town."

Ronny came out of the house. He was eleven and a half, and as usual, he was in charge. The police arrived and told us we had to come uptown with them, because there was no adult around.

A nice lady from the corner said, "I'll take her. She doesn't need the trauma of going to the police station after all of this." I was crying because I thought I was going to be arrested for killing my sister. The police officers agreed, and took Ronny with them to the station.

The lady's name was Mrs. Allen. She was so nice, except she made me a tamale to eat. I'd never had one before, and when I tried it, it tasted terrible. I asked if I could have peanut butter and jelly or macaroni and cheese.

"Sure, I have both. Which one do you want?" she said. She gladly made macaroni and cheese and ate the tamale herself. It was the best mac and cheese ever. I was still pretty shaken up, so we played checkers on a big rug that had a checkerboard printed on it.

Soon Ronny came over to get me.

"Were you arrested?" I asked.

"Nope. I got to ride in the police car and even turned the lights on! I ate some chips from a vending machine and got to get the dispatcher cigarettes from the cigarette machine."

I was so jealous. It reminded me of the tavern down the street in Chicago where my mother would send me and my brother, to buy her cigarettes and gin. All we had to have was a note.

"Is your mother home now?" Mrs. Allen asked.

Ronny said yes, and thanked Mrs. Allen for watching me.

As we were walking home, my brother told me that Mom was drunk, but she'd gone to see Rachael at Morris Hospital. I didn't like my sister much, but I felt bad because it was kind of my fault she was in the hospital.

When my mom got home later, she told us Rachael was doing okay but they needed to keep her there for a few days. She picked up some clothes and returned to the hospital, staying by Rachael's side day and night. If it had been me, she would have picked me up when I was ready to be discharged.

Mom did take the time to yell at me.

"You're a stupid idiot! You were supposed to be watching her. What the hell happened?! You're gonna get a beating when I get home. Your sister could die because of you!"

"I'm sorry, she just let go of my hand!" I started to cry. "I didn't know she was planning on running in front of a car!" I was afraid. I needed support and none was given. I've felt guilty about this my whole life.

CHAPTER 11

Who's Going to Take Care of Us?

After the accident, my dad had a lady named Lola take care of us. My mom said she was four hundred pounds. I had never seen a woman so big. My mom was skinny and pretty, so this was weird. Lola lived with us full time.

"You know, Lola is in love with Dad," my mom said.

I was puzzled. Why would Mom let Lola live with us if she was in love with our dad? I knew where babies came from, so I was worried.

"Will they have a baby together?" I asked Mom.

"Dad isn't in love with Lola. He's totally in love with me, so I'm not worried."

Later, though, Lola put the moves on Dad, and soon after, she was gone.

Great-Grandma Annie sold her house in Kentucky to come back and live with us again. She was surprised by a lot of our "newfangled" appliances. She still used a cast iron skillet to cook, and made pies and canned vegetables from her garden, which she planted herself. Secretly, I thought she loved the place. The only problem was, she thought eight p.m. was a good curfew and always locked my twelve-year-old brother out.

He solved the problem by unlocking the window before he left. He would get home late and crawl through the window. Great-Grandma Annie always assumed he was home the whole time. He got into some mischief. He was with the "wrong crowd" until they broke into a school and mom reeled him back in and grounded him.

Mother, can you hear me now?

*　　　*　　　*

Aunt Bindy came to visit, wanting to see JoJo and Grandma Annie. who had moved back in with us seeeing her daughter, she realized how much she missed her. She decided she needed to get out of Chicago and move in with her daughter. But she had no extra money. She asked my mom if she could move in with us, offering to clean the house and take care of all the kids.

My mom thought it was a great idea. Bindy could live with us for free, and my mom wouldn't have to pay a housekeeper. Grandma Annie had gotten to the point where she was unable to keep the house anymore, and she had trouble understanding us kids as we started to rebel. Soon after Aunt Bindy moved in, however, Grandma Annie threatened to move out. According to her, Aunt Bindy "cussed a lot and spent her time reading Harlequin romances instead of taking care of the kids." So Bindy cussed at Grandma Annie, who decided to go and live with her son, Uncle Shorty, in Chicago. She'd had enough.

Eventually Bindy wanted to go back to work. She took a typing test for the prison and unfortunately, she failed. There was also the problem of driving. She had PTSD from an incident that happened in Chicago. She was stopped at a red light when a man ran up and broke her window and snatched her purse. The man tried to get in the car but Bindy ran the red light and was hit by another car. She wasn't hurt, but she was scared. She got a ticket for running the red light. They never did find the man who'd done this to her. She was afraid to drive after that, and didn't drive for thirty years.

*   *   *

Soon after Rachael got out of the hospital, she and I were sent away for the summer. We went to Missouri to be with Rachael's dad, the one I call my "second dad." My first dad was my bio dad, John; my second dad was Rachael's biological father, Stan. Bill, my mom's current husband, was the one I called "Dad."

When we got there, Stan wasn't home. He was out driving a truck. (At this point, I thought when you grew up, you became a truck driver.)

Stan's wife Jeanine was there. She thought she was Loretta Lynn, and asked me if she sounded like her when she sang "Coal Miner's Daughter." I wanted to say, "No, you sing like a cow," but that would have been rude and it would've hurt her feelings, so I said, "Yes, you sound exactly like her."

She also couldn't cook. She would attempt to make biscuits and gravy, but they tasted like thick paste on cardboard. She also tried to make potato soup. It was just water, potatoes, and hamburger. It was all gross.

Rachael and I shared a bed with Jeanine's son, Stanley jr. We were all little, so it wasn't weird or anything. Their daughter, whose name escapes me (I'll call her Jenny), slept in a crib next to us. We were packed in like sardines. We'd all play together in the red clay during the morning, painting our bodies and faces to be silly. That game ended after two days when Jeanine had to bathe us each twice.

Jeanine was plain, but sort of pretty in a "girl next door" kind of way. She always wore jean shorts and T-shirts. She used to say, "You know, I dated George Harrison of Beatles fame." I didn't know anything about the Beatles, but I still thought, "Sure you did." I just tried to stay away from her, because although she could be nice sometimes, she had a temper, and she'd yell at me. Mostly she was nice, which brought back memories of my mother. My mother was nice sometimes, too.

I sought Jeanine's affection and admired her, even though she was often distant. Jeanine took the twelve dollars my mother had given me and used it to buy Loretta Lynn and Patsy Cline albums. I didn't really like their kind of music. Even so, Jeanine told my mom that I loved it.

Jeanine would have Clyde stay over when Stan was on the road. Clyde was a farmhand who worked there when Stan was away. She'd move Rachael, Stanley jr., and me to the floor in the living room, where we were supposed to sleep. She was so loud, how could anyone sleep?

At least Jeanine didn't beat me, which was a plus. I guess I don't blame her much; she was only twenty-seven, and she was lonely.

When Stan came home, I was lifted up to see inside his truck. It was very big and tall; you could see a lot from up there. I could see the blur of the cows in the field. (I didn't get my much-needed glasses until I was ten, so everything was a blur at that time.)

When he opened the door and I looked down, I said, "I'm too scared to get out."

Stan held out his arms and said, "Jump—I'll catch you." I seriously doubted his words, but with no other way out, I jumped right into his arms and he caught me. I began to trust him. I grew to love him, and was glad I got to visit when he was around.

Stan showed me how to milk a cow. It's an art. You can't just squeeze the cow's udder. You must squeeze and pull down at the same time. Soon I got the rhythm and it was easy. I watched the milk flow into the bucket. This was a little scary because I thought the cow might kick me, or the bucket, and in trying to dodge the kick, I'd knock the bucket over.

I noticed the flies liked the milk. Although we tried to shoo them away, there were always a few that ended up in the milk. We'd take the bucket into the house and set it on the floor. I wanted to drink the milk right away, but Jeanine told me we had to wait until the cream settled on the top. Then we'd scoop the cream off and refrigerate both.

I thought the cream would be ice cream. Not so. I was told you could use the cream to make butter. What a disappointment.

The next day Jeanine and I were sitting on the porch.

"Jeanine, where did the chickens' legs go?"

"What do you mean?

"In Chicago we always had four legs from the chicken; where are the chickens' other legs at?"

She never answered me, just laughed and laughed and called me a city slicker.

I figured that was because we wore rain slickers in the spring, during the rainy season.

CHAPTER 12

The Devil in Disguise

Soon Stan had to go on the road again. They lived in a very small Missouri town of about a hundred people, according to Jeanine. No one else lived near our farm.

When Stan was away, Clyde came over to do the chores. He taught me how to drive the tractor, collect the eggs, and feed the horses and cows. I was afraid of the chickens. The rooster would always peck me on the butt and the hens would peck my hands as I collected the eggs.

When we wanted chicken for dinner, Clyde would kill a couple by grabbing them by their legs. He'd put their heads on the ground and stomp them off. They really do run around like "chickens with their heads cut off." I thought it was the grossest thing. Then Clyde would throw the chickens into a vat of boiling water to remove the feathers. I can't even begin to describe how terrible it smelled. Thus continued my fear of chickens.

Clyde had begun to groom me, at the age of eight. He promised me chocolate and soda if I would let him touch me under my clothes. I loved the forbidden candy and soda, not realizing that pay-up time would soon arrive.

They were building a shed on the property, and only the frame and the rafters were built. Clyde told me that during the war they used to make prisoners clasp their hands around a rafter and then hang there like that, unable to get down. I didn't believe him, and he said, "Let me show you." He hung me up there and he was right: I couldn't get down. He took advantage of the situation and shoved his hands up my shirt and then down my pants. I began to scream and he finally let me down. I immediately ran away and avoided him the rest of the day.

The next day he woke me up before the sun rose, saying "We are going to the barn." As we walked, I smelled the hay and cows all around. He said, "You chickened out yesterday. You still owe me."

"I let you touch me under my clothes—that was the deal. You hung me up like a prisoner."

"Well, today we are going to try something new," he said through gritted, rotting teeth.

I was scared, and wasn't sure what would come next.

He picked me up and put me up on bales of hay that were taller than me. I tried to wiggle down but the fall was too great. He pulled off my green pants and raped me.

He grabbed a chicken from the yard and stomped its head off. He let it run around just a bit and made me watch. Then he grabbed the chicken again. He held it over my body while it was still actively spewing blood. He let the blood flow all over me while I screamed. He even put the blood into my mouth. He rubbed the feathers on my body. He scratched me with the claws and rubbed them on my face. He then threw the chicken aside and wiped the blood off my private parts. I didn't know if it was my blood or the chicken's.

I was so afraid and grossed out that I threw up. He began sucking and kissing my private parts while touching his penis. Then he put his penis in my vagina and hurt me again. I felt like it was tearing me all the way to my belly button. When will this stop? Why is this happening?

These episodes were repeated many times that summer and over the next three summers, until I turned twelve and refused to go back. To this day, I am allergic to hay.

I felt such shame. I never told anyone because I knew I was a bad, bad girl. I feel bad to this day that I left my little sister Rachael to go there during the summers without me. I was too ashamed to ask her if the same thing ever happened to her. We don't speak as adults.

Mother, can you hear me now?

*　　　*　　　*

At age ten I started my period. I was lucky I didn't get pregnant from Clyde's abuse. Aunt Bindy taught me how to wear pads. At that time you had to wear a Kotex belt. You put the belt on, and the pad had long strings on the end that you would put through these clips. The clips poked into my skin and made me look like I was wearing a diaper. I hated them. Once in school the long strip came up out of my pants and everyone laughed.

Aunt Bindy said I couldn't use tampons because it would take away my virginity. I thought about telling her then what had gone on with Clyde. But when I asked her if she'd ever been "touched in her private parts as a child," she said, "My uncle Shorty, Grandma Annie's son, tried to kiss me once." I never attempted to tell anyone else.

Aunt Bindy was nice enough to attend some of my choir concerts, including one where I had a solo, and she came to parents' night. I was glad she took out her curlers and her Dippity-do was dry. She was more of a parent to me than my parents ever were. My mom stayed in Chicago while Aunt Bindy took care of us.

*　　　*　　　*

Aunt Bindy didn't know that when my cousins visited us, Mike, the older one, tried to have intercourse with me. He always asked me if we were doing it, as he didn't actually know how to have sex. This didn't stop him from attempting it almost daily. He was fifteen and I was eleven.

I came in late one night and all was quiet. This was unusual, so I snuck upstairs to lock myself in my room. I crept past the first door—all clear. Then the next door. Still good. Aunt Bindy's room was empty. The next room was mine. I shut the door quickly and was about to lock it when Mike appeared.

47

"Hello," he said. "Welcome home."

I was caught off guard again. He'd finally figured it out, and he raped me. I knew it was wrong but there was nothing I could do. I knew I could tell no one. No one would believe me, and even if they did, they would have found some way to make it my fault.

Except for Ronny (whom I now called Ron), that is. He would have killed him. Ron really didn't like the cousins, anyway, even though they were close to his age of fourteen and a half. The younger cousin, Samuel, ruined many dinners because he often came home high. He'd walk in and his eyes would be all red and he'd keep his head down so we couldn't see his face.

Dad would say "Come here and let me see your eyes." Sam would walk slowly over to my dad, hoping the eyedrops he'd used earlier had taken the red out.

"But I only smoked a little. Not enough to get high."

"Just go to your room," my mom would say.

I wondered why he was always making my parents mad. Dinner was tense after he came home like this, and it caused me much anxiety.

When my parents weren't around, Aunt Bindy was clueless, or else she didn't care enough to stop him.

It was great when Mike and Samuel went home after the summer. I made sure I had to work detasseling corn the following summer when they came to visit for two weeks.

CHAPTER 13

White Boots

My mom and dad were still staying in Chicago during the week. Dad was on the road most of the time but came home when he could. Mom was supposed to come home on weekends but didn't unless Dad was home.

Roxy seemed to have a sixth sense when it came to Dad. Whenever she expected him, she would always look out the window toward the driveway. Within thirty minutes he would show up. We told her she had ESP. "Where is my ESP?" she would ask. She thought we were spelling Pepsi.

On Easter Sunday my dad would rent a private dining room for all of us at the local mansion, now turned restaurant, called the Lodge. It seemed to take forever to order and even longer to get the food. When the food finally came, three waitresses dressed in black smocked dresses delivered it on big trays. I would have dropped the tray, so I was glad I wasn't serving.

When the food came my dad asked the server to "hold his cigar." She politely took it from him and held it. He picked up his utensils and began to eat. She looked uncomfortable as she held the cigar while my dad continued to eat.

My mom laughed. "The poor girl has to go back to work, Bill. Take your cigar back."

We all laughed then, including Dad as he took back his cigar.

These fancy dinners took place only at Easter. Most times we ate at home because there were so many of us, and we were brats.

*   *   *

One night I was asleep in my bed when my mom came and woke me up.

"C'mon—get up and put this on."

It was 10:30 p.m. She was never home at this hour. I noticed she was very drunk, and high on top of that.

I got dressed as she instructed. I was wearing a midriff halter top, a see-through skirt with no slip, and my tall white boots.

"Mom, why did you pick out these clothes? I look like a hooker." I was eleven.

"Just meet me downstairs."

We went out the door and I saw a strange car. Mom was behind me, and she said to the guy in the car, "Okay, I'm giving you my daughter—now give me my stuff."

Drugs changed hands and I was pushed into the back of the car. The man got out his door and moved into the back with me. I knew what was coming, so I started fighting.

He said he liked it that way, so I decided to lie there like a dead fish.

I felt his heaviness upon me. His breath stank of cigars, onions, and alcohol. The inside roof of the car had a tear in it. I stared at this while he was on top of me. I could hear cicadas. They seemed to get louder and louder. My mind kind of left my body.

When he was done, I was a mess, physically and mentally.

I hurt "down there." I no longer trusted men. I guess I trusted no one. My past experiences told me to trust only myself. And maybe not even that. I felt like I had a big red "A" on my forehead that said "Abuse me." I felt used and abused by both the man and my mother. Who loves you and protects you if not your own mother?

My mom continued to trade me with this guy for years. She tried to get me to take the pill, but it made me sick so I stopped taking it.

My mother and doctor both knew the pill made me sick, so the doctor encouraged me to use condoms.

"Why is your daughter sexually active at this age?" the doctor asked at one of my appointments.

"She's wild—I can't control her," my mom said. "She just does whatever she wants, and I work, so I can't be around all the time. I'd make her a chastity belt if I could, so she would stay out of trouble."

The doctor looked at me. "Do you want a bad reputation?"

"No," I muttered.

"You need to quit having relations with boys," the doctor said sternly.

"Okay." I was embarrassed and sad and began to cry silent tears.

"I don't want to see you back here," the doctor said in a raised voice.

CHAPTER 14

Kids, We Need to Talk

About this time, around 1972, five years into her marriage to Bill, my mother decided she was going to divorce him. She and Jim Champion, the new man in her life, took Ron and me to a fancy restaurant with paper lamps and candles on the table. I kept feeling the tablecloth. I liked the silkiness as I ran it up and down my arm. We talked about nothing for a while.

Mom started with a tentative voice. "Kids, we need to talk. It's important. Jim and I have fallen in love and I am going to divorce your dad."

"You can't," I whined. "He's adopted us as his kids." Bill had adopted Ron, Rachael, and me just a few years before. Roxy was already his child.

Ron just sat there looking glum.

"Well, Ronny, what do you think?" Mom asked.

"I think you don't care about my opinion. I think you already made your decision," he said, trying to keep his face passive.

"Mom, if you divorce Dad, I'm going to live with him," I cried.

It was Thanksgiving Day and they had driven to Kentucky, where we were visiting for the holiday, to tell us. Maybe they thought I'd make a scene.

I was extremely upset, and so was Mom's sister, Bindy, her brother, Lee, and her mother, Nanny. Bill was the only dad I wanted. My mom had been having an affair with Jim Champion, who was my dad's best man at their wedding.

Nanny finally talked her into staying because of us kids.

Mom would always push Bill away when he tried to hug or kiss her. He was totally in love with her. Many years later, when he died of the famous thief of memory, Alzheimer's, at the age of seventy-four, my mother finally realized she did need him. She missed him terribly.

*   *   *

The sheriff called from Kentucky and said Uncle Luther had been shot. He was Great-Grandma Annie's son. He was sixty-one. It was decided by the police that it was a suicide, but we knew better. You don't shoot yourself in the head twice with a shotgun. In addition to this, there was a lot of money missing, along with his gun collection. The sheriff just said he must have sold it and loaned people money, but no one corroborated this story. However, the sheriff had a new car within the week.

Luther was a veteran. He was buried with honors at the family plot on a hill behind the "big gate." It wasn't a cemetery, just a burial ground on Grandma Annie's property.

Around this same time Uncle Shorty's son, my cousin Marcus, went to jail. Next step, prison. He was involved in murder, rape, aggravated battery, and many other felonies. He was in Menard Correctional Center in Illinois. I don't know if he is alive, dead, or free today. His name doesn't show up on the inmate list for Illinois. Great-Grandma Annie sure had her share of sorrow.

*   *   *

In 1974, when I was twelve, Aunt Bindy was pregnant by her boyfriend Dane. He was JoJo's father, too. They never married; he only came around for sex. I found out later he was married to someone else. I only met Dane twice, and never met his wife.

When Aunt Bindy went into labor she had to wait for my mother to come from Chicago. She needed a ride to the hospital and someone to stay with her through the labor and birth, so my mom told me to stay with Aunt Bindy until she got home.

During her labor I kept asking if she needed anything, repeating that sentence about every five minutes. She always said no.

"Does it hurt?" I inquired.

"Only mildly," she replied. "I was supposed to have a C-section next week but I went in to labor early."

I asked her what she was going to name the baby.

"I don't know. It depends on if it's a boy or girl."

"I want a boy," I told her. "There are too many girls around here."

"I'd like a boy, too," she said quietly. "But if the baby is healthy, it doesn't matter."

To my relief, my mom soon arrived and they went to Morris Hospital. My mom called about seven hours later and said, "Bindy had a boy. She had to have a C-section, as the baby was too big at seven pounds."

Aunt Bindy's first child had had a stroke when she was born and ended up with cerebral palsy. The C-section this time was to prevent this baby from having the same problems JoJo had. Bindy was tiny even though she was a very big eater.

My mom told me the baby's name was Thad Ronald, his middle name in honor of Ron, the only boy in the family. Although Ron was the "Golden Boy" who could do no wrong, he was becoming annoying. He hung out with the popular crowd—Karl, Mike, and someone else I can't remember. He became kind of stuck-up, in my opinion.

CHAPTER 15

Junior High

Although I was teased when I was in junior high, I wasn't really bullied too much. Once when I was in gym class a girl stole my bra. I had big boobs and needed the bra because I was wearing a body suit—a top that goes over your head and snaps at the crotch. It was tight-fitting, so I couldn't go around without my bra. I called my house and said I was coming home because I was sick. I got a note from the office secretary. This was before they had a nurse in the school.

In PE class the girls had silly activities like rhythm gymnastics. You danced with a ribbon, or holding a ball, girlie things like that. Every class started with a song and exercises that wouldn't make your muscles too big. You stuck your arms back and pushed out your boobs and sang "Go go chicken fat, go away." It was some sort of fitness song written in 1962, and used for years after.

I dated a sixth grader, Ken. He was nice. I was teased for dating a sixth grader while I was an eighth grader. We got in trouble when we were caught kissing while babysitting.

My friend Beetle and I went to visit her grandma in Indiana. We liked the boys we met there, and started dating. When I got back I told Ken it was definitely over between us. He was crushed. I felt badly, but I was going to high school the next year, and as a freshman I wanted to date older boys.

Once I rode my bike to the Dairy Queen. I didn't know it, but I would be passing Colleen's house. I was jealous of her; she was so pretty, and was one of the first girls to get boobs. I had big boobs, too, but she was pretty and wore makeup.

When I rode by that day, all the popular girls were outside Colleen's house.

"What are you guys doing?" I asked.

"We're practicing our cheerleading for the new pee-wee football team," Colleen said.

"Oh, okay. Good luck."

They didn't reply.

Of course they're cheerleaders, I thought.

They hadn't held any auditions, just kept it real quiet. My friends and I thought this was horrible. We would've liked to be cheerleaders, too, but we never even had a chance.

The next day I was walking around town and spotted a crowd of teenagers. I walked up and asked if I could hang around with them. They laughed at me and said, "Go away, stupid little junior high kid." One of them threw a rock at me and it hit me square in the head. I started bleeding profusely. I went to the dime store and asked for a rag. They saw the blood on my face and took me home. Mom and Dad were both home, which was odd.

My dad took one look at me and said, "Let's go to the doctor. I think you need stitches."

I promptly started crying. "Can't you just fix it?"

"Come on, just get in the car."

My dad was very patient as I trudged toward the car. Needless to say, I received stitches.

*   *   *

One day I wanted to go to the high school football game.

My mother said, "No, I think you should stay home."

"Please," I whined. "Everyone else is going."

After much begging my mom finally let me go.

The Athletic Field stadium—or A-Field, as we called it— was about two stories high. I was running when I fell from the top all the way down, hitting my head on the concrete wall. My neighbor Harry was standing close by and he came and wrapped me in his arms and ran me to the car. He took me home. I had a huge bump on my head.

When Harry brought me to my mother, she yelled, "I had a mother's intuition about this. I really didn't want you to go. Now see, you've hurt yourself."

Harry was still standing there. "I think she needs to go to the hospital," he said. "She had quite a fall and was disoriented afterwards. With that big bump, I think she may have a concussion."

My mom just looked at him and said, "She can use an ice pack right here, and I'll make sure she doesn't go to sleep."

I was using the ice pack when I fell asleep two hours later. I slept for the whole day and part of the next. There was no further treatment or any discussion of going to the hospital.

*   *   *

All through grade school and junior high I'd loved to play four-square. This is a game where you use a rubber ball and try to get to square "A" from square "D," bouncing the ball to each opponent and trying to get them to miss the ball. If they missed, they were out and went to the end of the line, back to square "D." I was very good at this game and occupied square "A" most of the time. It made me feel like I'd accomplished something. I knew it was a recess game and not something people were usually proud of, but I had so few things that made me feel proud. I had very low self-esteem and took every bit of praise I could get.

We also played tag, and chase. Chase is where you chase the cutest boy and he runs from you until you tag him. I don't know what we thought we would do if we actually caught the boys. These were junior high boys who didn't want to be caught by the emotionally mature girls. In a few years, the chaser would become the chased.

*   *   *

Sometimes Mom made pot roast with all the fixings for supper. I loved that meal. Other times she would make steak, which I also loved. I thought it was unfair that my brother Ron would get a whole steak while my sisters and I had to share one. Mom always made spaghetti when I was around, saying I loved it, when in truth, I hated her spaghetti.

I don't cook at all. I can make two things well: mashed potatoes and, you guessed it, spaghetti. I don't use my mother's recipe.

I really can't cook. Some of my "famous" dishes include taco pot roast, exploding hot dogs in the microwave, and caramel brownies you can't get out of the pan, and even if you could, if you put one in your mouth your jaws would never open again. Also, my famous fudge. One time after I made it, it didn't set up. I brought the cookie sheet in and told my friends to gather round, giving them each a spoon.

I also managed to catch the microwave on fire once. I had bought some hot dogs that were wrapped in plastic and some bits of metal. I knew nothing about taking them out of the package and cutting slits in them. I put the hot dogs in the microwave, which promptly arced and caught fire. I pulled them out, blew out the flame, washed them off, and served them cold with potato chips.

Mom and Ron usually sat at opposite ends of the table. Mom and Bindy made sure an adult sat between the younger kids, in case one might choke. Luckily, I was seated between my sisters. One ate meat and the other vegetables. It was easy to pass food under the table. Or we just "accidentally" dropped it on the floor for the dog, Chivas Regal. Of course we had a dog named after alcohol.

CHAPTER 16

Not Such a Good Idea

In 1975, when I was thirteen, I ran away with my friend Lisa. I packed mostly Kotex as I was on my period. I made a major goof when I forgot my glasses. I am blind as a bat without them. I first got glasses in fifth grade when I started failing every class. I was always in the back of the room, with assigned seats, and couldn't see the board.

Lisa and I were about a mile outside of town when the police came by. We threw ourselves down in the snow-covered grass to hide. We didn't realize we were going the wrong way to California. We were unknowingly headed toward the women's prison outside of town. I just remember lying in the snow until the police went by, and then having to get through fences every so often. When we got as far as the prison we decided to go back home. We were scared we'd end up there.

When we got back home our mothers laid into us.

Mom yelled, "Where did you think you were going?"

Somehow I had developed a bad habit of laughing when I was really scared.

"Do you think this is funny?" my mom screamed.

I said, "No not at all." I began to shake to hold in the laughter. I tried to keep a straight face.

"Why did you do it?" Mom asked again.

I replied, "I had a term paper due tomorrow and I didn't have it done."

This was way before Google. You used encyclopedias to write papers. We didn't have any, so I had to go to the library. The books were lined up by number according to the Dewey Decimal System. The librarian was a bitch who looked like she had just walked through a fart. She questioned why I was there on a school day. I told her school was canceled, then just shrugged my shoulders and told her to call my mom.

The next day it snowed hard and school was canceled. In Illinois it can be 80 degrees in the morning, so you wear shorts. By the afternoon it could be pouring, and by the evening, we could get a couple inches of snow. We have two seasons in Illinois: winter and construction. There are a few days of spring and a few days of fall.

I remember on this particular snow day it was incredibly cold. Every place was closed.

I put on my snowsuit and decided I would walk the six blocks to Dairy Queen for a treat.

It was closed. Imagine that.

*   *   *

I had a transistor radio that I loved. I read books and wrote while listening to the "Big 89" radio station, with Larry Lujack and Tommy Edwards, also known as "Uncle Lar and Little Tommy." They had good songs, and played trivia and other games. Uncle Lar would promise Little Tommy a "shiny new dime" if he got the right answer. They also played "Animal Stories," which was funny but dark. We'd listen to the Cubs on WGN on my radio during the day. The Cubs had no night games at that time. I still love talk radio.

I also caught lightning bugs at night in the summer. I'm not proud of the next thing we would do: We tore the lights off the bugs and made bracelets with them.

When I was in junior high, I was still in Girl Scouts. People liked to buy Girl Scout cookies from little kids, but not from junior high kids; even so, I sold 120 boxes. People loved Thin Mints, and the price was lower by far than it is now.

Mother, can you hear me now?

*　　　*　　　*

I was a freshman in high school in 1976, and went to prom with the past year's prom king. I was envied by some of the girls, because usually you couldn't go to prom unless you were a junior or senior. My date's name was John. Another girl named Lori thought he would ask her, but he asked me instead. I don't think Lori ever got over it. John and I dated for a few months after that, but he was a farmer and in the fields from sunup to sundown. I had no patience with being ignored.

I also dated a boy from the Methodist youth fellowship group. His name was Don. I sat with him and his buddies at lunch and watched as they played cards. They didn't care for me that much and he soon broke up with me. It wouldn't have been so humiliating if he hadn't done it at lunchtime. I cried all day and into the evening, but eventually got over it.

That same school year, I was asked to raise the basketball hoop. I climbed up the ladder and started to use the Z-shaped crank. It was very heavy and my arms got tired. This resulted in the crank slipping and hitting my index finger. The fingernail immediately turned black and purple and was gushing blood. I scampered down the ladder and ran to find the gym teacher, trying hard not to cry. Until I saw the gym teacher, Miss Dayton. I cried behind her closed office door as she applied pressure to my finger—my nail was a goner—and call my house.

"Hello, this is Ms. Dayton. Is Bindy there?"

Aunt Bindy had answered. "Yes, it's me."

"Emory has had an accident at school and needs to come home."

"I'm so sorry—I have no way to come and get her. I have other kids at home, and I don't drive."

"It's okay," Ms. Dayton said. "I have a study hall next period; I can bring her home."

When I got home my hand looked fine so Bindy did not seek medical attention.

CHAPTER 17
The Things We Do for love

My brother had gotten married when his high school sweetheart, Alice, got pregnant, nearly two years before. He was a senior and she had graduated the previous year. They had a baby named Jeremy. He was so cute.

I wanted to take Jeremy to see a Bugs Bunny movie but his mom said he couldn't go until he'd eaten all of his roast beef. He ate the last bite and we left right after he'd put on his shoes, walking to the Blackstone movie theater a couple of blocks away. He was too small for popcorn so I bought a small bag of candy for us to share. I was getting ready to give him some when I noticed he was chewing something. I took it out of his mouth. It was a gristly piece of roast beef! He was so relieved he could now have pop and candy.

When I was fifteen, I started dating this boy, Bruce. He was my sister-in-law Alice's brother. I spent hours getting ready for our first date, choosing what to wear. I couldn't decide between Love's Baby Soft or Avon's Sweet Honesty perfume. I finally decided on a pair of white bellbottoms with a brown blouse, which showed off my boobs and blonde hair. I can't remember where we went. He gave me rides to and from school. His parents were somewhat strict so he wasn't allowed to have me over. He did come to my house to pick me up and drop me off. My parents were nice to him, but liked my previous boyfriend better.

I thought I loved him. No, I knew I loved him. I'd fallen hard, and in my mind was already planning our future wedding. I decided I wanted to have consensual sex with him. It was a new feeling for me, to not be scared when men were around.

Before long I was pregnant. I asked Alice to tell my mom. I was too scared.

One day, I felt wetness in my underwear. I was not wearing a pad and thought maybe I wasn't pregnant and had just skipped a month of my period. I went to the bathroom and saw a lot of blood. There were some sticky, stringy, bright red clots. My stomach was cramping. I told my mom. I wondered if I had miscarried. She said she would take care of me. She said because of these issues my baby would be retarded, if there was a baby left.

We went to Chicago when I was six weeks pregnant. The doctor called me in, and my mother talked to him. They decided to "take care of me" by doing a D and C. At the time I didn't know what this meant. In those days people weren't as open as they are today. I hadn't had my first high school health class yet, so I wasn't really sure about all the stuff surrounding periods and babies.

They had me take off all my clothes and put on a gown with no underwear on. I was embarrassed. They told me to get up on a gurney, which the orderly pushed to another room with a very bright light. They told me to slide over onto a skinny table. They put a mask on me and I fell asleep. I felt weird when I woke up. I didn't ask any questions. On the way home I asked my mom if my baby would be okay now. She told me that the baby was taken care of and was gone. I cried all the way home.

I went home and told Bruce. He was livid that I'd gotten pregnant, and blamed me. He soon got over it and we went back to having sex.

Four months after the loss/termination of my baby, I became pregnant again. Alice took my urine sample to the doctor and then, per my request, told my mother. I told Bruce, who then broke up with me.

I was determined to keep my baby despite everyone's objections. Bruce denied he was the father. My mother voted for abortion. My friends Jeanine and Deeann thought adoption might be a possibility. I reiterated that the baby was mine and I was going to keep him no matter what. Some other girls, Mary and Vicky, told me to go to an unwed mothers' home like they had, where they gave their babies up. They said no one would know.

That's strange, I thought. The whole school knew about you gals.

My mom was friends with Alice and shared a lot of secrets with her, but only if they didn't put Mom in a bad light. She never told Alice how I'd been abused in the past, and how she'd neglected Ron and me.

Alice and Ron eventually divorced. Although they only had one child together, Alice was still considered a member of our family. Poor Alice would go on to face many challenges in later years, including cancer. She always maintained a good attitude.

Years later my brother got married again. He and his second wife tried to have children for years, and lost their first baby during her second trimester of pregnancy. They went on to have five more children, including a set of triplets. She was a good mom.

CHAPTER 18

Unexpected Pregnancy

During the first few months of this pregnancy I missed most of my first-hour algebra class because I was puking in the bathroom. Another teacher, Mr. Bucks, wouldn't let me sit sideways in my desk, even though my stomach didn't fit. The gym teacher made us do sit-ups. He got mad at me and said I wasn't trying. A few months before, I could do forty-five per minute. Now I was doing only ten. I still remember his face when he heard me say "I'm five months pregnant now!" He came to me, his head down, and he looked truly sorry and apologized to me. I can't even remember his name now, but it was so touching.

One of the teachers, Miss Coulter, taught English. She was terrific: She did cartwheels in class and talked about her cat, Miss Mousey. She let me talk to her after class. She told me it was my right to have tutors come to my home if I wanted. While I appreciated the information, the last thing I wanted was to stay home. I wanted to go to school, to be with my friends while I still could. I loved Miss Coulter; she was everyone's favorite. She gave teachers a good name. She was the kind who treated everyone as if we were the adults we desperately wanted to be.

In school, I was seen as "slutty" from then on. The "bad girl" who was only sixteen and pregnant. This was especially true when they heard my boyfriend, Bruce, tell other people that the baby wasn't his. I guess they thought I slept around. I had dated only Bruce for a year—who else could be the father? I'd never come close to dating anyone else, much less having sex with them. He was the only person with whom I'd had consensual sex at this point in my life. I felt embarrassed and ashamed, but adamant that I was keeping this baby.

*　　*　　*

For as long as I can remember, I've loved to write. I've filled up reams and reams of paper over the years.

No one ever asked me what I was writing. Either they didn't care or didn't notice. I think they just didn't want to face what I was writing about—all the abuse, my feelings and thoughts about people. Whether there was a God, and if so, where was he in my life?

I was never seen without a clipboard of paper or a notebook. I hate to use the word notebook because kids nowadays think of an electronic device; same with tablet. Actually, I often used a steno pad. Most people don't even know that a steno pad was originally used for taking shorthand. Not like OMG or WTF, as people use now, but rather a way of taking down notes using symbols, sort of like the wingdings font. Most people can't read it, and most of those who knew it have forgotten it now.

I was also never seen without a book. To say I read a lot is an understatement. I read a book every one to two days. I generally don't read books a second time. In fact, if they change the cover of a book and I happen to buy it again, I'm ticked. It's not only the money wasted, but losing the thrill of knowing I have a new book to read.

I don't know what directs people on what books to buy. Some say it's the cover; others say the first few pages. I choose a book based on its plot or subject matter. I buy a lot of books about cultural experiences. It helps me learn something new while also entertaining me.

I can't say I have a favorite book; it depends on the genre. I never knew how to pronounce that word until I heard it in a movie.

Books are comforting. They are friends, they are knowledge, and they bring a deep sense of satisfaction when you gain familiarity in the topic. A sense of belonging and becoming the characters. Of touching others' lives—of feeling you are not alone in yours.

*   *   *

I was on the flag squad at the homecoming football game when I ran into a boy I had dated when I was a freshman. His name was Donny. I had been distraught when he left me freshman year. When I met Bruce, the father of my baby, I felt I knew what love was. Then I was devastated when he left me, too.

Donny returned when I was a junior. When I told him I was pregnant, he still wanted to date me. I think he had a "Prince Charming riding in on a white horse to save me" personality. It was admirable. At first.

He went home and told his parents, and his dad's advice was: "Keep it in your pants. She may be trying to trap you."

Truth was, he'd already had it out of his pants.

His family was well respected and well off. My family was middle-income, and from the wrong side of the tracks. Soon after we started dating again, he asked my mom if he could marry me. I was only sixteen, so he needed permission. She gladly gave it with the stipulation that we wouldn't get married until after the baby was born.

I thought it was nice that he'd talked to my mother before asking me. It showed a bit of respect for her. She deserved respect at this point, as she was sober when he asked.

His parents thought I was ruining his life. I think he wanted to rebel against his parents. What a way to do it. His father, Lloyd and my father, Bill, both refused to talk to me for the entire pregnancy. My mother's response was to flirt with Don; he was oblivious. His mother sent me Bible verses in letters. I got jealous when my husband wrestled with my beautiful skinny sister, Rachael.

Mother, can you hear me now?

My future husband was nothing to write home about. He wasn't cute, but he was good in bed, and he's aged well.

CHAPTER 19

Motherhood

My fiancé Don was staying the night at my house—separate bedrooms, of course—when I awakened him with a shake. "I think I might be in labor."

"Go tell your mom." He was nineteen and didn't have experience with things like this.

I went downstairs and told Mom, "I think I might be in labor." It was 2:45 a.m.

"Make me some coffee," she said. To her credit, she'd gotten home early that night and was sober as a judge.

At 8:00 a.m. we drove to the hospital. Don had a panel van which only seated two, so my mom sat between us on the floor, smoking cigarette after cigarette.

Fifteen hours later, my son was born. I had a high forceps delivery, so he looked like a conehead. The nurses assured me this would go away. Initially I didn't think David was cute, but in a few weeks he was adorable. He was named after a great Christian man in my church, the man I most respected besides Bill, known as Uncle Dave.

Suddenly, both fathers were talking to me again. I had given them a great gift, and they were so proud.

Don and I got married three months later. I began to closely align myself with my husband's family. They were well respected and most of all, normal. I thought if I was connected with them, I would be normal, too.

After David's birth I went back to school while the baby spent his days with Aunt Bindy. I rushed home after school to see my baby, and when he went to sleep, I did my homework. I had to work hard to graduate as a junior by taking correspondence courses and extra classes.

I got the solo in the spring concert that year, but didn't want to stay late at rehearsals. I wanted to get home to baby David, so I lost the part as a result. I didn't mind; motherhood was the most important part I'd ever play.

Aunt Bindy would watch him in the middle of the night so I could sleep. I tried to breastfeed, but he ate so much I couldn't keep up. We switched to formula and he drank a quart a day. He was eight and a half pounds at birth and very soon topped ten.

David was three months old when Donny and I were married in 1979. My mother set up the whole thing. I had a "pastel rainbow" wedding where the girls all wore a different pastel color—ivory, rose, green, yellow, and peach. My sister Rachael wore the peach. She was eleven. My mom said she had to be in the wedding or my parents wouldn't pay for it. I don't know what life was like for her. I was always jealous of her naturally rail-thin body and cute face. For being a short person, she had beautiful legs. We never really got along, and this has carried over into adulthood.

Eighteen months later I had a daughter, Brandy. Sixteen months after that I had another daughter, Amanda. I got pregnant again right away and had a miscarriage. The doctor said it was twins. I was severely depressed. But two years after Amanda was born, I had a son, Daniel.

*　　　*　　　*

Although I was living my dream of motherhood, it was lonely being a new mom with a baby. All my friends were still in school, and Don was busy with his job at the local factory, Cartel Papers. They made phonebooks and newspaper circulars. He was either working or sleeping. He worked nights.

I simply talked to David like he was an adult. He learned to talk and walk early. Once when we were in church, I put Brandy on David's lap. He was twenty-two months at that time, and she was a heavy baby. He yelled out, "Mom, you put her on my penis!" The whole congregation snickered.

71

Another time, the preacher was saying a rather long prayer and even I got bored. David yelled out, "Say 'Amen,' I'm hungry!" The whole church laughed that time, because they felt the same way. The preacher stopped and said, "Okay, David, I'll stop."

The next week at church, David called out loudly while looking at a woman, "Mom, look at her. She's so fat!" The woman and I were both appalled. I made him apologize. So, he said, "I'm sorry you're fat, lady." Then he crawled under the pew to the end where she was sitting. He said, "She has her shoes off and her feet stink so bad. Maybe she farted?" I was mortified and immediately took him out of church.

We went to the bathroom so he could go potty, and I made him stay with me while I breastfed his sister. We were sitting on the floor when he asked, "Why is she sucking your boob?"

"That's where the milk comes from."

"I want to try some," he said.

So I got him a cup and expressed some milk.

"Is there a chocolate boob?" he asked.

"Nope, only white."

He took a taste and said, "You better give Brandy a bottle. That milk is sour. It tastes blech."

CHAPTER 20
life Changes

Don and I moved through life as most young couples with children do, managing kids with no time to really form an "adult" relationship. My husband was tired of working in the factory so he applied to the police force. I also wanted something to do besides singing nursery rhymes to my kids and collecting pop bottles for Dairy Queen money.

In 1985, I applied and was hired by the village's volunteer ambulance service. I received very little pay—about five dollars an hour, when I was in the ambulance. I received nothing if I didn't get a call. It was my spending money. I got the job; Don didn't. It was possible he didn't get in to the police force because David's bio dad, Bruce, worked as a police officer and there would have been a possible conflict of interest.

Don continued working at the factory and provided well enough for me to stay home with the kids. Money was tight, but we made it. I had my money from the ambulance service so I could buy a few things without having to ask my husband. Don watched the kids when I had a call. If he was sleeping or working, I had my cousins Jo or Thad, Aunt Bindy's children, watch the kids for the hour and a half that the call usually took.

I don't know whether Don was stressed or just realized he couldn't handle another man's child, but he started treating David badly. Both my mother and Don's pointed this out to me, but what could I do? Most of the time Don worked overtime and then slept all afternoon at home. It didn't take long for our marriage to take a nosedive.

I became friends with a woman named Marsha from the ambulance service. Don became friends with a woman at work named Kara. We would divorce the following year, and he and Kara would get married a few months later.

Although it sounds petty, I was hoping she would dump him. Even though the divorce was mutual, I wasn't ready to be thrown away so easily.

*　　　*　　　*

I was working nights at the Harvest Table, affectionately called "The Hole," and had JoJo, Thad, or a friend named Valerie watch the kids.

One night when I was off work I got a call from the restaurant.

"Emory, I need you to come out here," Carrie said.

"But I don't work tonight," I replied.

"It's something else. We don't want to call the police."

Thinking they couldn't reconcile the cash drawer or something, I put my clothes on and went out into the snowy night. I took the time to warm up the car even though it was less than a half-mile away.

When I walked into the restaurant, I went straight to the cash register.

"Is that your mom over there?" Carrie asked.

I looked and said, "Yes, that's my mom."

"Well, I'm sorry but you need to get her out of here. She's drunk or on drugs. She got up a little while ago and went over to the plant in the corner and peed right there in front of everyone."

"I'm very sorry," I said. "I'll take care of her."

I walked over and slid into the booth across from my mom.

She looked surprised to see me. "Well, hello, Emory babe." She called me that when she was drunk or stoned, but never when she was "normal."

"Hi, Mom. I hear there's a bit of a problem," I said evenly.

"Nope, I'm just having supper." She smiled.

"Mom, you're making a scene." I spoke in a nonthreatening manner. If I confronted her about the drugs and alcohol, she would start screaming.

She didn't say anything, just picked up her whole steak with her fork and chewed around the outside.

I did what I always did in these situations: I called Ron.

He was at the restaurant in ten minutes. I told him the whole story and he looked mad. He was a redhead and had a temper. He went over and sat across from Mom.

"Oh, how nice it is to see you, Ron," she said. "Did someone tell you I was here?"

"Emory called me."

Mom looked at me and said, "Narc. You want me to look bad in front of my favorite kid?"

I said, "No, Mom. I needed his help to get you home."

She wanted to finish her meal so Ron cut up her meat for her so we could get her out of there faster.

At least I was familiar with the night shift. Drunks came in all the time and I served them. When they were too drunk to speak properly and I couldn't understand them, I simply ordered them a Trucker's Special: three eggs, bacon, hash browns, and toast.

The next day, my mom was in the kitchen, drugged out again. She was trying to cook pinto beans. She kept trying to stir them but she was too close to the pot. She damn near caught herself on fire.

I said, "Mom, let me handle the stove. You are too drunk or high; it's dangerous." I nudged her away.

She pushed me and I pushed her back. She was so drunk she fell into the laundry basket in the next room.

"I have to stir the beans!"

"You are in no condition to be anywhere near the stove," I said.

"I have to stir the beans!" she yelled again.

"I'll stir the damn beans. You need to leave this house now. I'll take care of the kids and finish up supper. If you want to slowly kill yourself, fine! But don't keep your kids in a mess that is not their fault. Leave this house now!"

She left. Probably to go to some bar.

She came home the next day. She wasn't remorseful, nor

had she understood my point. Did I mention she was drunk when she got home?

*　　　*　　　*

In the midst of this, Mom had been planning to take some courses at the local college—one of her attempts to "do better."

The next week when she started class, I thought she would straighten up and stay away from drugs and alcohol. I was wrong.

On her way home she drove her car into a ditch. The car was totaled. Problem was, the college was north of town, meaning she passed Dwight on a route she wasn't supposed to be on and ended up in the ditch west of town. No one in the family was told she'd been cited for DUI. This was before they put that information in the paper, so I found out about it from the police.

CHAPTER 21

Rachael

My sister Rachael was getting married. We the kids and I had to come home early from vacation because Rachael wanted my daughter Amanda in the wedding.

After the wedding, my mom flirted with the groomsmen. She unzipped the back of her dress and was holding it together with her hand while she talked to them. She'd rub their chests and squeeze their shoulders, saying things like "If only you were older or I was a teensy bit younger, the things I could teach you." I was relieved my sisters weren't around at the time to see her acting like an easy sleazy.

Rachael and her husband had a baby boy. He was six weeks old and holding his head up. She put him to bed that night and the next morning she was surprised that he had slept through the night. She went to his bassinet and he was lying facedown. She turned him over and to her horror, he was red and purple. He had died sometime during the night. The coroner called it SIDS, a term we had never heard before. My sister was relieved to learn that it wasn't her fault. I think she still feels guilty even though she went on to have three more children.

My birthday was on the sixth of July, Rachael's on the seventh, and my uncle Doug's, the eighth. We never celebrated on the sixth, only the seventh. I never had my own birthday. Rachael knew we'd be decorating the hall for her wedding, scheduled for the seventh. She had arranged for everyone to get presents for me and surprise me with my own birthday party, on the sixth. It worked; I was surprised. I'm so grateful to her for that.

Rachael's future mother-in-law was busy decorating and helping my sister while our mom just sat there, drinking and complaining of chest pains. It made her look like an ass.

"Can I take you to the emergency room for your chest pain?" I offered.

"It's not that bad," she said.

We all just ignored her and continued decorating.

In Mom's defense, she was sober the next day, for the actual wedding.

Rachael never looked more beautiful.

CHAPTER 22

Ambulance Service

I learned everything about being a good emergency medical technician (EMT) from my new friend from the ambulance service, Marsha. I also learned that women could be brave and strong. Marsha was married but didn't have to listen to her husband. I thought all women had to listen to their husbands—that their word was law—and let them do all the thinking. She taught me so much. She made me feel good about myself.

This was a new feeling for me. I wanted to impress her in everything I did. She'd turn around and I'd be carrying all of the equipment I could hold. She would just shake her head, like They are giving me kids to work with. I was twenty-three. It was 1985.

I went on an ambulance call once on Christmas. It was one of the few times I was without Marsha's guidance on a call. The person had crashed his car and was deceased. That really got to me, because I knew before his mother knew. I knew it would ruin Christmas for the family ever after. I never got over that one.

There was another call where three guys were riding motorcycles. One went over to the side of the road and drove into the grass to stop himself. Unfortunately, there was a manhole cover just lying there beside the road, and he hit it. He flew off his bike and hit the guardrail with his head. By the time we got there, he was DOA (dead on arrival). His buddies wanted us to "zap" him. At that time EMS did not carry defibrillators, so we couldn't zap anybody. These men kept getting closer and closer to us and were acting threatening. We finally had the police move them away from us.

We examined the body and determined that he had died on impact. There was no change in the dirt below his mouth. He did not breathe after he hit the guardrail. He had been gone too long, about fifteen minutes. A call was made for the coroner. It was such a surreal experience. It was dark, and all you could see was the ambulance and officers' lights and the angry faces of his friends.

Accidents have a different feel to them. We were called to another scene where two semis had collided. Both drivers died. It was dark, but lights were flashing all around us and traffic had been stopped because the road was blocked. People on the other side of Interstate 55 were driving slowly to try to see the accident. Gawkers. We all do it. Sometimes people watch sports or racing just to see if a car will crash or a person will get hurt. It's normal, but annoying to EMS personnel.

There was the smell of diesel fuel, blood, and dirt at this scene. We were worried that there would be a spreading fire as the engine on one of the semis was smoking. When it was light out, some of us went to see the burned-out semi, to try to piece together what happened. Sometimes it just doesn't make sense.

During another call, when the police got to the scene of the accident they told me to stay in the ambulance. I peeked around the corner and saw a man who looked like my brother, Ron, lying dead on the ground. I looked at the car and it was the same kind my brother drove.

I asked the officer if it was my brother. He said "No."

No problem, I thought. I can do this.

I received the coveted stork pin for delivering a baby in the ambulance.

The lady had walked slowly toward the ambulance, holding her stomach. "The baby is early by a month," she said. This was in the thick of winter, and it was snowing heavily.

Uh-oh, I thought. My first time delivering a baby other than my own, and it's a preemie in a snowstorm in the back of an ambulance.

I checked her and said, "This baby is ready now. Just try to breathe through the pain."

I remembered that breathing never seemed to help my concentration when I was giving birth, but decided at least one of us should be doing it. I put oxygen on her and pulled out the birthing kit. Gloves, masks, scissors, clamps, and a blanket. I then removed her panties and saw a tiny head readying itself to be born. I wasn't ready, the mom wasn't ready, but baby was.

She gave a few pushes and a tiny baby boy slipped out into my gloved hands.

"It's a boy!" I pronounced.

I gave the baby oxygen and wrapped him in a blanket, then in another one of those space blankets that look like they're made of aluminum foil, to keep him warm. I had his mom hold him close under her shirt. It was a cold winter in Illinois. Although I delivered mom and baby to the hospital in stable condition, I was saddened to learn that the baby died ten months later following a seizure.

Once we had a call that had seven victims: four young people in one car, and two adults and their baby in the other. The baby and parents made it, but two people from the first car died. Another guy in the backseat of the first car was going to college on a track scholarship; he had two broken legs, and was upset his career was over before it got started. There was a girl in a green coat that we pulled off the guy with the broken legs. She did not respond and was clearly dead. I asked another EMT to watch her in the ambulance. For some reason I didn't want her to be alone.

If you have a massive accident like this one, sometimes you turn to the gathered crowd and enlist help until other medical professionals arrive.

I asked the crowd, "Do we have any doctors or nurses here?"

Nope.

"Any medical personnel of any kind?"

Nope.

"How about a Boy or Girl Scout that has had first-aid training?"

A man stepped forward.

I asked, "Do you have the stomach for blood, guts, and death?"

"I was in Vietnam," he said.

"You're hired. Here—hold this bandage and apply pressure."

He did great.

All living victims were transported to the hospital while the others left in a hearse after the coroner had pronounced them dead. Sad.

There was a local place called the Wheel Inn. It was for indigent people, and quite run-down. We were called for a "foul odor coming from a room at the top of the stairs." Wherever the EMS goes there seems to be a crowd that follows. This crowd had been told to stand back, away from the porch and steps, as they had been deemed unsafe.

I had a weak stomach for some things, and indeed, there was a "significant odor" coming from the room. The hallway smelled like body odor, cigarettes, and piss. But when the door to the room was opened, the stench that hit my nose made me gag uncontrollably. I stood at the door and looked at the body on the bed. There was a copious amount of old, alcohol-smelling vomit. Most people when they die will lose control of their bowels and bladder. This person must have had a lot of bowel contents, because it was not only on the bed but across the floor as well. The body had been decomposing for a few days in the humid 90-degree Illinois weather.

I ran from the room, down the hall, and down the stairs. I ran outside and promptly threw up over the side of the porch, straight onto the bystanders. The crowd dispersed and moved closer to the curb, waiting for my next retch. I watched from the porch as the body was removed. My stomach began to roll again, and I doused those who'd been curious enough to move back to the porch. We had warned them to move back in the very beginning, so it was kind of their fault.

At another call there were five victims. The guy in the backseat had his eyeball hanging out. I decided to let another technician get that one. I started CPR on one of others, all critical. After they'd left in all the ambulances we had available, Marsha and I, sitting in the ditch, both burned out at the same time. We had done CPR thirteen times that year and none of them made it. We realized we'd been left at the scene and had to call a police car to come and pick us up.

After that we no longer wanted to take calls, go on ambulance runs, or attend continuing education. We had flamed out, pure and simple. We weren't offered any debriefing from the stress of the "bad calls." There was no talk of PTSD for health-care or EMS workers. We resorted to dark humor with each other. We'd go to the local twenty-four-hour restaurant and talk and laugh to drive away the ghosts that robbed us of "normal emotions" and ate into our comfortable lives. We put on the masks that carried us through our "regular lives," but the demons still haunted us in our quiet moments.

We'd go home and strip off our clothes, putting them right in the washer to remove some of the blood, gasoline, and grime from the accident scene. We'd shower to remove the devastation from our minds, checking ourselves for glass, dirt, and grime. Blood has a distinct smell, and once you get it up your nose, it stays with you for a while, following you when you step back into your "sterile world."

Yet somehow, even though we no longer went on calls, part of us still craved the adrenaline rush. We had "pager reflex." It was so bad the fryers at McDonald's made us jump and reach for our pagers.

CHAPTER 23

Marsha

Marsha was amazing. I wanted to be around her all the time. I realized I loved my very best friend. We started holding hands. When I sat next to her on the couch, I felt comforted and safe for the first time in my life. I realized this was a strange relationship.

She got divorced. She and her husband, Steve, were great friends; it was amicable and took no time at all. Don and I had been separated for a year by this point. Division of property and visitation took a while to decide, and it only made sense for Marsha to move in with me and the kids. It was nice of her, as she didn't really like kids. She would sit in the smoking section in restaurants so she didn't have to sit with kids. She didn't hate my children; she tolerated them and learned to love them. In the early years I'd ask her why she stayed, as I knew kids were not her favorite. She would simply say, "Because I love their mother."

I worked at the local factory, the kind of job that makes you realize you don't want to do it forever. I would take these square coils and put a cut in both sides. It was piecemeal. I always hit my daily quota, and then some. I wanted to make sure I received those bonuses. Sometimes I worked the line. Parts would roll by fast or slow and everyone had a "piece" of it to do. I put epoxy on the coils. It was boring.

Another time I worked the big green machine, making cruise-control buttons. It was a mindless and thankless job. I didn't work there long and never made any true friends. I was very lucky that Marsha would watch the kids on her days off, Friday through Monday. My friend Jeannie watched them the other days. Jeannie knew I was strapped for cash so she charged me very little.

I quit the factory job because I wasn't making enough to cover my sitter, and I missed my kids. I stayed home and babysat for a family who had three kids, all maniacs. These kids liked to break things. Their mother kept coming home later and later, and with four of my own children to care for, I couldn't stay up till one in the morning every day and still get up early to get David to school. We mutually decided that she would find another sitter.

I spent my days watching soaps, especially General Hospital and One Life to Live. I had to find out what was happening in Eterna and see what Luke and Laura were up to. I found my kids enthralled in these stories, too. I know it was nonproductive and a general waste of time, but it wasn't my only activity. I also continued to read, and kept writing in my spare time. Reading and writing—they go hand in hand.

*   *   *

Because my jobs didn't work out and I needed the money, and couldn't afford a babysitter, I asked Marsha to watch my kids while I went to college. We talked about what profession would make the most money in the least amount of time. Dental hygienists make a lot of money but rarely have insurance and benefits. Registered nurses make a great deal of money and have benefits. At that time, RNs could practice with an associate's degree, which amounted to two years of nursing classes and one year of prerequisites. I decided to go for it.

While I found nursing to be interesting, it was also very difficult for a person like me. I had no credits from high school that could be transferred into college credits. As much as I was concerned about this, I was eager to learn. I made many new friends, their ages ranging from eighteen to forty-five. Women just out of high school, single ladies, pregnant women, moms who had four and five kids, widows, and two men. We were a melting pot of differences and similarities.

I remember being scared when I couldn't make hospital corners on my beds, and having to do exams on my fellow students. Learning to give shots by practicing on oranges; how to use many of the IV pumps and starting our first IVs; and the scariest part of all—an instructor named Joan. She was known for failing students in their last and most difficult semester. Critical care and ICU. However, she made the nursing boards easy. After she was through with you, you could do anything in nursing. We were the smartest we'd ever been.

What started out as "the fastest way to get through school" became a profession I loved. There were so many ways to use a nursing degree, and I've tried most of them.

Marsha and I decided that when I finished school I'd buy her a car. She agreed, as she was driving the carpool in a Chevette. I reminded her that there was a method to the school drop-off and pickup routes. The other mothers would get mad if you did it wrong.

She figured she could do it another way, so the first day she tried it doing the route backwards. All she got was yells, honking, and a couple of middle fingers.

She came home and said, "Those mothers are crazy!"

I silently thought I told you so.

It looked like a clown car when she dropped off eight kids, my four and my best friends four at school. Children came out of this small car with all their gear. She was made fun of all the time. Especially when her clutch went out. The crossing guard at the school knew not to have her stop because she'd never get going again.

CHAPTER 24

Is This love?

I had a revelation in 1986, one year after I'd met Marsha. I was feeling close to her, but didn't really understand. I started having thoughts of kissing her as we were lying on the couch. I asked her if she'd ever had any sexual feelings toward me and she replied, "Nope, not a one."

The next week was her birthday. We were in the car and she said, "Ask me that question again."

I was not going to look stupid. I said, "No way."

"I might have changed my answer," she said.

We had these silly grins on our faces the rest of the night. We laughed through the whole supper at Chicago Dough Company restaurant. I'd taped an episode of Oprah that featured a lesbian. When we came home that night, we lay on the couch together to watch it.

After the show was over, I said, "What did you think?"

She said, "I think we might be more than friends."

I said, "I think so too. I've never felt this safe, or as close to anyone. You are my protector."

She kissed me. My lips were tense and firmly closed.

"You're going to have to relax if this is gonna work," Marsha said.

I relaxed and it was wonderful, but still confusing.

Was I gay? I couldn't be. I'd been married, had kids, and was a good Christian woman. This was against God and his word, the Bible. What was I going to do?

The next day I went to her house to tell her this could never happen again. She stood up and walked over to me. She kissed me and my knees went weak.

I was saying to myself, I'm not gay. Maybe bisexual, but not gay.

After a few days of kissing her, I thought, Yup, I'm gay.

I realized that I'd been in love with her from the first moment I saw her. I told her I loved her, looking deep into her blue eyes and running my fingers through her black hair. You aren't taught how to make love to a woman. We fumbled our way through it. Thus began the greatest love story ever written.

Marsha replied, "I don't just love you—I'm in love with you."

That scared me. She was using words only my husband had said to me.

For the next few years, I went back and forth, praying that God would take this affliction from me even as I found I couldn't resist her. Something about her made me fall more in love with her every day.

I think women fall in love with their heart, soul, and mind, while men fall in love with their stomach and sex with a good-looking woman. That's why you'll see a fat, bald man with a hot woman. You rarely see a hot man with a homely woman.

*   *   *

As bizarre as my childhood was, Marsha's was the polar opposite. She was "raised by a village."

"What exactly does that mean?" I asked.

"It means things were simple. My mom didn't have fancy names for me and my brothers Jim, Joe, and Tom. She was a woman of few words, except when it came to me. We would gossip for hours. Not really gossip, because it could be about people she didn't even know. She was the first person I told things to, because I knew she would tell no one. She never had a bad word to say about anyone.

"Being raised by a village means there were no privacy fences. Everyone knew their neighbors. You could play in anybody's yard even if they didn't have kids. Every adult had the right to discipline you, and news of your wrong-doing would arrive home before you did. Everyone was on good terms. I automatically waved at an older lady's window before and after school even if I didn't see her in the window. If I didn't, she would call my mom and ask if everything was okay.

"I had good parents. My mother was a saint, but my father was more into himself than others, including his kids. He received free meals in the Colonial Room at the University of Illinois in Champaign–Urbana. It was pretty fancy. Because of this, he never took my mom out to dinner. When I got older, I took her out all the time."

Her mom Clare had cancer and died way too soon. Basically, the last year of her life she was in a coma. After a year, she "woke up."

Marsha asked, "Mom, is there anything you'd like to do?"

Clare said, "I hear there's a new Walmart and Sam's Club. I'd like to go there. Also, there's a movie called Sister Act I'd like to see."

"Okay, Mom, we'll do that tomorrow."

The next day we went to Sam's Club. Her mom went straight to the candy aisle. She started pulling Milky Way candy bars off the shelf and putting them in her cart.

"You must really like those," I said.

"I've dieted my whole life," Clare said. "Now I'm going to eat whatever I want."

"Good deal," I said as I gave her a knowing smile.

Marsha is a very intelligent person. She had the highest score in the nation on her national boards of dental hygiene. She has a wicked sense of humor. She read encyclopedias as a teen. She has a photographic memory and has read almost all the books in the library.

She dated a very nice man named Dennis in college. She broke it off as gently as possible. Soon, she met Steve, the man she was going to marry. They were engaged for two years before marrying. They had a lot in common. They were best friends and were married for several years. Eventually, she broke up with him. He couldn't hold a job, and as we became closer, she realized had to end it with him.

Marsha isn't a deep thinker. When someone says something, she takes it at face value. She never thinks, "I wonder what they meant by that?" I, on the other hand, am the exact opposite.

Marsha has a childlike quality to her. She loves everything and everybody. It's so easy to make her happy. If you gave her a pile of manure, she'd be happy with it and use it to fertilize her garden.

I, on the other hand, hate surprises. I hate holidays like Thanksgiving and Christmas; they hold only bad memories for me. I hate opening presents. I always got weird gifts that I didn't want. One year I got a knee-length maroon coat with no zippers or buttons, only a belt to keep it closed. The pièce de résistance was the fur around the collar with an animal head on it. I hate acting like I love the gift when in reality I hate it.

I usually go into a deep depression from Thanksgiving to after New Year's. First of all, the weather is usually dark and dreary, which I hate. But it's not just a seasonal depression; it's a debilitating one. I know that the holidays are going to be the worst. It's like a swirling vortex of despair and a dark cloud of black death. I just sit in a chair and ignore my personal hygiene. I don't go out of the house. I don't want anybody asking "What's wrong?" and then trying to take their advice that won't work for me.

I think I have gotten better over the years with extensive medication changes. I am finally on the right meds and have far less episodes. Also, Marsha has learned a lot from my years of counseling and time spent in psych wards. I am grateful she took the time and effort to go to counseling with me and visit me in the psych ward. Most of my counseling sessions were related to mom's neglect and the abuse I suffered. Most of the time, Marsha explained things while I cried.

CHAPTER 25

Church

The kids and I continued going to the Methodist church during these years. In a prayer request once I asked for prayers for our family, as money was tight with only Marsha working. I also requested a visit from the pastor. Neither request was granted. Someone at the church told me I was seen as an embarrassment. Personally, I think it was because Don and his family went there. Don's parents gave a lot of time and money to the church, so I feel the church chose money over my children's needs.

We stopped going altogether. No one called. Former friends evaporated. I was so hurt, I never even looked for another church, as I'd been judged so harshly by some of the Methodists.

*   *   *

I had four kids, and Marsha didn't have any.

My oldest son David was very hyper and difficult to raise. My oldest daughter Brandy was a spitfire. She was my child of rage. Amanda was very sweet, but a bit of a tattletale (although this usually worked to my benefit). Daniel was a little clueless, but was definitely the baby of the family.

Most of the time Brandy was helpful, but sometimes she would say, "I want my own room!" That was our cue to run out the front door, hoping she wouldn't ask one of us to give up our room. And you could never ask "Are you on your period?" She usually was, but that really set her off. She would whip her long brown hair around and her head would spin just before she started beating you senseless.

91

I swear her eyes would change from gorgeous blue to demon red.

And then there was Amanda . . .

One time when we were in Chicago two tall black men entered our elevator. Amanda asked, "Why are those men—"

"Hush now," I said, thinking she was going to ask, "Why are those men black?" (We had no black people in our town.)

She began again, "Why are those men so—"

I pulled her close and squeezed her shoulder, saying, "People don't talk in elevators. It's the rule. You just look up at the numbers and not the people. We are all strangers, and we don't talk to strangers."

The men smiled and got off the elevator.

I was mortified, and then surprised when Amanda finally said, "Mom, I have to know—why are those men so tall? How can I get that tall?"

We are a family of short people, so I understood her need to know.

I also told her that there are many different colors of people and everyone is equal in God's eyes.

*   *   *

One night we got a frantic call from Amanda, who was babysitting.

"Mom, there's a car sitting outside with its motor running and its lights off."

"Okay, give us directions," I said.

Marsha and I were wearing our short purple summer pajamas. We just threw T-shirts on over the tops and grabbed a baseball bat and flashlight and left the house.

Soon we arrived at the farmhouse where Amanda was babysitting. We saw the car in the driveway. No lights and the motor running, just as Amanda had said.

Marsha rushed out of the car in her T-shirt and silky purple shorts, with me close behind. She walked over to the car and threw herself against the driver's side window, shining the flashlight in the driver's eyes and showing the baseball bat.

The kid shouted, "I live here! Don't hurt me!"

Marsha said, "You'd better go and tell my daughter who you are, and make sure you never do this again. You scared the shit out of our daughter, who's in there babysitting your sister."

Marsha was an imposing figure even in purple silk shorts.

*   *   *

My youngest son Daniel was definitely the baby of the family. He was only one year old when Marsha came into our lives and spent a lot of time with her when I was in school and working. As he got older he often said things like "Marsha does everything right." Other days I'd come home and he would be in full camo makeup. I'd ask, "What did you learn today?" He'd say, "Not to backtrack when dropping off the bills." I was hoping he'd say he learned his colors or numbers. Marsha had never been around kids, so I told her the things she should be teaching him and how to do it. She did get better. I loved her even more because she began to love my kids. I think you earn brownie points with a woman if you love her kids and are willing to be a good parent to them.

When Hippie Day was approaching at school, Brandy and Amanda just went to Marsha's closet. They wore circular sunglasses, their long hair parted down the middle, fringed vests over tie-dyed shirts, and some bellbottoms and peace necklaces. They won first place.

That was the only time anyone wore anything from Marsha's closet, as she's not the fashionista I am. She would come out wearing long red shorts and tall gray socks with blue stripes on them, with a blue tee. She saw nothing wrong with this.

One time we were at a softball game and Daniel came running across the field dressed just like Marsha. Everybody was laughing so hard as they asked whether Marsha had dressed him that day.

From then on, I was the designated clothes buyer. I would buy Marsha Garanimals for adults. I folded the outfits together for her but she still got to choose what she wore.

Occasionally I'd send her back to the closet and make her change.

CHAPTER 26

Commando Parenting

Like most parents we were busy all the time, trying to keep up with all four kids. I'm sure there are more stories than the ones mentioned here, but we probably don't want to know.

One time they made Kool-Aid with all the available sugar in the house. They poured it on their cereal. Marsha came in the room and saw the mess all over the counter and floor. She was livid.

Three-year-old Daniel had a poopy accident. He was covered in poop down his legs and had Cheerios and Cheetos stuck to his butt and legs. The floor was so sticky you could take your shoes and put them on the wall and they would stick. Marsha took Daniel outside and hosed him down, then took him, shivering, inside and gave him a robe and diaper. She wasn't good at diapers. They were always loose and easy to poop around. After a couple of poopy diapers, out of desperation, she learned the proper way to do it. She still put her shirt over her nose and mouth and gagged while doing diaper changes. Daniel considered Marsha (he called her Moo) his best friend, and he thought it was an honor for her to change him. Marsha thought differently. To this day, Daniel remembers Marsha pulling her Snoopy shirt over her nose and mouth and gagging. I wonder if this is why Daniel does the same thing with his kids.

Daniel decided to run away when he was still in diapers, wearing nothing but hiking boots and a diaper. He went and opened the door and as the wind whipped around his little legs, he came back into the kitchen and said, "I'm running away upstairs." The next time Daniel decided to run away he was about five. We got out our biggest suitcase and packed it with a huge candle, two pairs of hiking boots for when he got older, some wood to start a fire, and a bunch of other heavy things. He was small and had to swing the suitcase around to pick it up. He walked outside with it but kept looking back. He couldn't see us from the alley. He got just to the end of his boundaries and two of the biggest dogs he had ever seen leaned over a six-foot-high fence and said "Woof!" What we knew—but Daniel didn't— was that the dogs were standing on picnic tables. He came trucking back toward home dragging the suitcase the whole way. He came into the house and said, "There's danger out there!" He never tried to run away again.

One week, Daniel and Amanda said the F-word at church. We got to the car. Daniel was sitting in the front seat between Marsha and me. He said, "I don't have to listen to you." We gave a response I'm not proud of, both of us thumping his head at the same time, boink-boink, side to side. He was quiet all the way home. Amanda knew when to keep quiet.

*   *   *

One summer when he was around eight years old, Daniel got a new protective cup to wear when playing baseball. Marsha got him a jock strap. I knew nothing about these things. She said, "Never buy a small jock strap because they will grow into it. Plus, a small size would embarrass any boy."

Our friends Kathleen and Carolyn Jury ran in the same circles we did, because our kids were best friends. Kathleen had just bought her son his first protective cup. He was in right field and was squiggling all around.

"Kathleen, I think your son might have to pee," I said.

She looked at him doing the squiggle dance.

"I think you might be right; I'd better check."

As Kathleen walked to the fence to ask him, he saw her and ran over. He reached down his pants leg and took out the cup.

"I can't play with this thing."

Kathleen just put it in her pocket, something only a mother would do. I guess it's better than walking around holding it.

As we had four kids playing baseball and softball, plus Marsha and I played, we went to thirty-seven games in one month. Daniel told us, "At Grandma's they have bowls of food on the table and you can take as much as you want."

"I think you just described a meal, son." I felt guilty, and didn't take hot dogs home from the ball park for a few months.

If you don't know, the game of softball is the national sport for lesbians. We meet there, we cruise there, we fight there. We fall in love there; we fall out of love there. We meet friends and lovers and ex-lovers.

One day Marsha and I were at a softball game with some friends. We decided to count ex-girlfriends. Vicki had seven, Julie had fifteen, but Bonnie had too many to count. I asked where the first baseman came from and someone simply said, "Bonnie's house." A simple statement, but true.

One night we had a baseball game for David, one for Brandy and Amanda, and one for Marsha and me. Marsha and I dropped the kids off at their games and left for ours. Our adult team was undefeated, easy wins as we were all die-hard competitors. One girl on our team played with broken fingers and one with a broken wrist.

We coached softball. We didn't know who the kids were, so when the coaches picked, I got all the younger kids and those who were new to the team. We had to teach these kids everything. How to throw, hit, and run bases; the rules and positions. One of our girls hit the ball and promptly ran to third base. Another girl cried in the outfield because she was "lonely and scared." Her older sister played on the team as well. We simply told her, "If the ball comes to you, pick it up and throw it to your sister. That's all you have to do is throw it to your sister."

I guess she decided her sister was too far to throw to, so when she got the ball, she walked it to her sister. We yelled, "Run, run!" So she handed the ball to her sister and then began running around the bases. A few concepts were missed.

There was a young girl on the team who lived with her grandma. She was from Tennessee. When she was in the batter's box, we kept calling over to her to hold her bat up. All she did was lean farther over the plate. After several attempts at instruction we called a time-out and went over to her. I showed her what "bat up" meant. She looked stunned as she said, "I thought you were saying 'Butt up.' " The crowd tried not to laugh.

We had a great pitcher. Her name was Lori and she was a natural. She saved us from complete disasters and shutouts. We didn't win many, if any, games, but the girls learned a lot. The next year we did better when a girl named Stacy played for our team.

Once we left to go to our game after dropping the kids off at their games. When we returned, Marsha went to David's game while I went to Brandy's. I noticed Brandy had incredibly large gray pants on. She was trying to hold them up and bat. She got a hit and she ran with her left hand holding her pants while her right hand was on her helmet, so neither would fall off. I wondered what the heck was the matter.

I walked to the other field and saw David barely able to breathe or bend over in his pants. I pulled both kids to the restroom and made them switch pants. They complained when Marsha went with David to the boy's bathroom to do the switch. After the pants were changed, Brandy could run, and David could catch.

*   *   *

Brandy and Amanda's room was always a mess. Our friend Vicki came over to help so we could all go for pizza. A relatively new but good friend, she was our key into the underworld of lesbians. One day she decided to help the girls while Marsha helped the boys and I did laundry. Vicki only had a son, so she was in complete shock when she saw all the different kinds of Barbies. Suntan Barbie, regular Barbie, Doctor Barbie, Nurse Barbie, Malibu Barbie, Safari Barbie. They had all different kinds of shoes and boots. She finally came to me and said, "Do you know how many shaved-headed Barbies and accessories I matched today? I quit! It's not worth a pizza."

And they wondered why I chose to do the laundry.

CHAPTER 27

David's Troubles

From the ages of sixteen to eighteen, David was known for drinking to excess and going to all the parties. One day he crept out his window onto the porch roof and dropped to the porch rail.

Marsha was sitting on the bench out there, smoking. "Fall out of bed?" she said.

He just went back in the house.

The next weekend she was sitting in the window and noticed him putting a cooler under the porch. She waited awhile and then went out and confiscated it and hid it in the basement. She watched as he came back looking for it. He never did find it. Just walked around, looking puzzled. Who was he going to complain to? Certainly not us.

Another time he put the cooler on the porch roof. Remember, we lived on Old Route 66, a main road, so many people passed our house to get to the store. In addition, Morris Road was in front of our house, which was the way home from the pool and the park. Lots of folks called us and said, "Hey, there's a cooler on your roof. Thought you'd like to know."

We did know.

Marsha had taken the cooler when David went to school and poked holes in all of the cans and dumped the beer into the sink. She put the cans back so every time he checked, his beer was still there. He thought he'd fooled us. Not so with commando parents.

*   *   *

One night at three a.m. we got a call from the Dwight police. My heart stopped. They said they had David up there. I got dressed and rushed over. All six-foot-one of him was sitting in a chair and all five-foot-three of me walked over and hit him in the back of the head.

The officer said, "He didn't do anything wrong."

I said, "If I'm here at three a.m., he did something wrong. So, what did he do?"

The officer said he'd been with someone who did something wrong.

"The other guy is over eighteen so he's in jail. David was with him when he was bashing mailboxes in the country."

"David, who were you with?" I asked sternly.

"Edwin, the youth pastor, and Todd," he replied.

"Really? Are you nuts?" I said.

"I didn't know he was going to do it."

"You don't put yourself in those situations. If he had killed someone, you'd be in jail, too. Maybe even tried as an adult."

"I didn't think about that," he said.

"Okay, let's go home," I replied.

He said, "I can't. I have to bail Edwin out. He's in Pontiac jail. I have to go to an ATM and get six hundred dollars."

"Is he going to pay you back?"

"Don't know, but it doesn't matter."

That's the one and only time one of my kids was at the police department.

David and his best friend, Todd, my friend Kathleen's son, played serious football. Because the school found out the boys had spent some time at the police station, they had to sit out the game. It was Homecoming and Todd's mom and I had to watch the boring north entrance. We were the "bad moms." The price was $1, $2, $3, and free for senior citizens. It took Kathleen and me awhile to figure out what

Marsha was doing. The money didn't add up to what we had counted from the cars. We found out she was charging the over-sixty-five senior citizens money, but not the high school seniors. She had let them in for free. We explained the problem with that. She made it up with the next car of drunken teenagers when she charged them $20 to park.

*　　　*　　　*

Marsha and I tried to take the kids on weekend outings, sometimes staying over at motels. Once, David thought it would be funny to throw a chair into the pool. Not funny. We had to leave the pool. The other kids were mad at him for having to leave.

David was so smart, but he had a weird sense of humor. He would get under the table at the pizza place where he worked and bark at his friends. When we ordered pizza, he delivered it to our bedroom. We got used to getting a pizza with three pieces missing and a note on the cover that said, "Thanks, Mom."

Later, Brandy worked at the same pizza place and the kids there tried to prank her. She finally said, "I live with David. You can't scare me." They all agreed with her and said, "Good point," and left her alone the rest of the time she worked there.

David's dad and grandpa wanted to give David a BB gun. Marsha and I were vehemently against it. As a result, David shot out all his grandpa's windows on the north side of the house. He also shot at his brother, who ducked just in time to avoid losing an eye.

CHAPTER 28

Cars

I always put my four kids in rooms over porches so they could escape in a fire. I thought we should practice fire drills. One night the smoke alarm was making that chirping noise when the batteries are low. It awakened everyone. The kids came out and wondered what it was, and I told them it was the smoke detector.

They all yelled, "Fire drill!" David put Daniel under his arm and out they all ran to the meeting place at the pole in the alley.

Because of these drills I knew my kids were prepared. I was a great mom at least for those five minutes.

*　　　*　　　*

David was sixteen and driving home one day. He couldn't figure out why all the cars were honking at him and flashing their lights. Indeed, he had to walk past the driver's left front tire that was flat to get into the house.

Marsha walked him back to the car to show him why people were flashing him. She taught him how to change a tire. She tried to teach me just like my dad did years ago, but I figured I'd just call roadside assistance for help.

When Daniel was older, he was driving along when he saw a wheel pass him on the road. He thought, "Cool, a tire"—just before the car went clunk. He called Marsha and asked what to do, and she simply said, "Call a tow truck."

Marsha and I had car paranoia. We thought every noise coming from the car meant the end of our vehicle. We had a car we swore was a two-cycle engine. We were always adding oil. We started it with a screwdriver. Marsha got good at putting the oil in fast. Once we were in East St. Louis in the middle of the night; she had the oil open and I stopped at a red light and popped the hood. She got two quarts of oil in before the light changed. What a woman!

Brandy never drove. In high school she was babysitting and the girl ran in front of a car. Brandy called me while I raced from work to the scene. I checked to be sure the girl was okay—she was already in the ambulance—and then went to see Brandy. She was calm and collected until I hugged her; then she cried. She hardly ever cries or allows anyone to hug her, even as an adult.

Adding to Brandy's driving anxiety, her brother David drove them to school. David was driving to pick up Todd at his grandma's house. Brandy's friend Carrie was leaving from her grandma's to pick up Brandy. Carrie pulled out blindly on Old Route 66 just as David was approaching from the other direction. They collided. Airbags went off and both cars were totaled. Thankfully all involved were okay. I was called at work and I threw my keys at my supervisor as I quickly told her the situation. I knew I couldn't drive under the circumstances.

Marsha had all my kids standing on the corner when we pulled up. She knew I'd be scared, so she wanted me to see them right away.

Brandy didn't drive until she had three kids who went to different schools and daycare.

*　　　*　　　*

Do you mow the lawn, or cut the grass? I mow; Marsha cuts. . . . Actually, I don't mow because I am allergic to grass. The boys hated mowing the lawn, so Marsha did it. The kids made sure they left plenty of rocks, kitchen utensils, and pop cans in the yard. Once she hit a rock and it flew and hit the house. The next time she mowed over a pop can, resulting in flying shrapnel. She had to come in and smoke a cigarette and get a soda while she calmed down. When the kids saw her, white as a sheet, they felt bad. After that, we hired out the lawn mowing to a neighborhood kid, Jason. He continued to mow our lawn until he was thirty and got a good-paying job. We loved him.

When it was 20 below zero and school was called off, the kids wanted to go out and play. Marsha told them they could. I looked at her like she was crazy. Marsha's mother, Clare, started to laugh. It took them all an hour before they'd found all their stuff. They went out for five minutes and came back in, saying it was "too cold to go out and play."

✻   ✻   ✻

One day as I was answering nature's call, the toilet wouldn't flush. Marsha tried for weeks with different plumbing liquids, coat hangers, and sandblasters. Finally, after a very brief discussion we decided to call a plumber. She lined the kids up and said, "I've called the plumber. He is going to pull the toilet, so you all better 'fess up, because he will find whatever is down there."

The girls looked guilty, so Marsha said, "Okay, girls, what's down there?"

They replied, "A comb, two toothbrushes, G.I. Joe, and maybe a dolly. We never saw her after the swim party."

Marsha said, "Okay, go sit on the foyer steps."

We never grounded the kids to their rooms because it was too much fun up there. On the foyer steps there was nothing to do except look at the avocado green paneling and untwist the burnt orange shag carpeting. Marsha heard them talking and went in and stared at them and they stopped.

Later on, after this plumber's visit, our toilet started to tip back. Marsha put my wooden cutting board below it so it wouldn't rock. We were good for a while, but then it started moving from side to side. Marsha's brother Tom came from Bloomington–Normal to try his hand with it. It worked for a while, then didn't work again. The kids went upstairs be-

105

cause they didn't like "Mr. Toad's Wild Ride" every time they sat down. Our upstairs bathroom had a pink toilet, tub, and sink. The boys hated it and were embarrassed when their friends came over and had to use this bathroom.

We had been attending our church, New Life Assembly, for six years. We asked them to pray for our toilet every week for nine months. One day Marsha lifted up a quarter of the tiles. She ripped until she'd found a three-by-three-foot hole. I happened to come in at that time and was horrified by what I saw. I had to look again to make sure. I asked, "Is that the basement?"

"No, it's the attic," she said. "They put the attic down here so the basement wouldn't flood." She laughed. "Time to call the plumber."

The plumber from My Father's Handyman came over right away. I asked the fee and he gave me a quote. It was steep for us, but probably fine for regular middle-income families.

The next morning the plumber called and said, "I've been praying about it, and the Lord told me to charge you half."

My prayers of the past nine months had been answered! A new toilet, and one we could afford.

The next day a young man came over, put in subflooring, tiled the floor, and fixed the toilet. It was beautiful! I told him we couldn't afford all that. He just said, "It's what's needed. I talked to the boss and he said, 'No charge for the extras.'"

I just stood there and cried, thanking him, and God.

Marsha asked, "How long did we have before we would've landed in the basement?"

"About an hour," he said.

CHAPTER 29

Mom, Marsha, and Me

My mom was always jealous of Marsha, thinking Marsha wanted to replace her. Mom always said I was looking for a mother figure, and I'd think, Mom, you are way off base with that idea.

Mom would call me every week. She couldn't understand why I never had time to talk, or if I did, our talks would always end up with someone crying or yelling.

My mom would open with, "I think you love Marsha."

I would say, "Of course I do. Look how she has helped me and the kids. Look how happy I am."

"No," she'd say, "I mean, you are in love with Marsha."

"So what if I am?" I'd say defensively. At that time lesbians could have their children taken away just for being gay, so I never fully admitted it to anyone unless I truly trusted them. And my mother wasn't to be trusted.

"You know, God hates gays. Remember Joyce who worked for me?"

Mom had always made snide remarks about gays and lesbians.

"Joyce is a lesbian dyke, and she's black."

I'd say, "So what's your problem with her—the lesbian dyke thing or the black thing?"

"Both," she would say, as if I should know and agree with this.

I disagreed on both counts.

My mom would come from North Carolina to visit and do all sorts of things to irritate me. Knowing my house was always a mess, she'd notify me two hours before she arrived. She knew this made me embarrassed and caused great anxiety. My house wasn't filthy, just cluttered with toys and a mountain of laundry.

Even though Mom and I were always at odds, I still needed and valued her. I tried to do things to get her to like me. In her own weird way, I guess she loved me; she's always act like she did when others were around. This confused me.

She knew we were on a strict budget. During one visit we wanted to take her out to dinner, and we chose Chinese because we thought there wouldn't be anything real expensive on the menu. We entered the restaurant and looked at the menu. My mom chose the most expensive item, which featured crab and lobster. It was twelve dollars, which at the time was quite pricey. We only had twenty-five dollars, so Marsha and I shared a meal and a drink so we would have enough for tax and a tip.

That night Mom went out to the bars with Ronnie's ex-wife, Alice, and came home drunk. She and Alice went out drinking a lot, which I thought was kind of disloyal to my brother. Mom slunk in to sleep on my couch. She didn't want Dad and Bindy to find out she'd been drunk. This happened many times.

Later, during another of her visits, we hid our car in a neighbor's garage and turned off all the lights in the house. We told her we had plans and wouldn't be able to host her on the couch. She became angry. She didn't want to be chaperoned by her husband and sister. Mom didn't want them to know how much time she spent in bars.

*   *   *

My nice neighbor, Mrs. Swartz, who was about eighty, let my kids play in her yard. One day we were playing flag football there, using dish towels tucked in our waistbands.

A foreign exchange student who was staying with a local family walked by, and the kids called her over. She smiled, and I asked if she wanted to play. She declined, saying she'd never played this game before.

We showed her how, but she was wearing high heels, so I went in and got my extra pair of tennis shoes. I told her to throw her shoes in the pile and put mine on.

She loved the game, but can you imagine what she went home and told her mother? "First you tie a dish towel to your shorts. Then the lady of the house gives you her shoes . . ."

*   *   *

For years we attended football and baseball games, band competitions and parents' nights, and color guard, as well as coached girls' softball, ran Girl Scouts, acted as treasurer for the Boy Scouts and ran their concession stands, along with many other activities that all parents do. Although Marsha and I remained the talk of the town, they didn't hesitate to let us do all the work typically associated with parent volunteers.

I must admit that when the father-and-son campout rolled around, I had to fight to be able to attend, as Don wasn't interested in going. The leaders were appalled that a woman would come to a Boy Scout camp. After all of that fighting I did for moms to be able to go, I must confess that I was a bit of a wimp when it came to camping. It started to pour, and another mother and I left our rain-soaked tent and moved to my car. I made a fool out of myself and set moms' camping with boys back to the Stone Age. My son, David, and the other boys just laughed.

CHAPTER 30

Boycotting

Marsha and I have boycotted several things over the years. Anita Bryant and her orange juice, due to her stance on gays and lesbians. She hated us. Then we boycotted Nestle. They were sending baby formula to Third World countries, which had to be mixed with water. The problem was, these women did not have clean drinking water, and the infant mortality went up until this procedure was discontinued and the women went back to breastfeeding. Then, we boycotted Pizza Hut because Rush Limbaugh was their sponsor. He called us femme Nazis, or something like that. My daughter Brandy was a picky eater but she loved Pizza Hut. She finally asked, "Can we go to Pizza Hut and eat and then tell them we dislike their sponsor?" As I had already written to Pizza Hut's administration, I relented.

*   *   *

At one point, we had a senior, a junior, a freshman, and a seventh grader in the house. We never slept. I made it a policy that if a kid wanted to talk, especially a teenager, you should listen, no matter the time, even if you had to get up in two hours.

One night we had a kid come in at midnight, and the others at two, three, and five a.m. We were exhausted the next day, but we ended up with happy and well-adjusted children. Well, happy, anyway.

Speaking of happy and well-adjusted children, here are a few of the things they came up with to drive us crazy, which led to our style of commando parenting. Which is probably why our sons both went into the navy. Boot camp was easier on them than we were.

When Daniel was a baby, I tried to sneak some medicine into his bottle. He took one drink and said, "Fix this," and threw the bottle under the couch. David picked it up and drank it. So, David slept and Daniel coughed. Ah . . . something that made David sleep . . . Hmmm, no, guess not.

Our girls looked nothing alike, except for their long hair. When Daniel was little, he couldn't tell the difference between his sisters. We didn't realize this until we asked him to take something to a specific sister; he looked at them for a long time and finally threw it on the floor in front of them. Then he ran away.

Marsha and I were gone for a few days. We called home to check on the kids. JoJo was babysitting.

"How are things going?" I asked Jo.

"Fine, fine," Jo said. "Everything is going well."

I kept hearing the kids laughing in the background, so I was convinced things were okay. I talked to the kids and they all said they were "being good and having fun with Jo."

I knew something was up, but didn't find out exactly what it was until we got home. Turns out Jo didn't have any dishwasher detergent, so she used Dawn dish detergent instead. She thought it would work the same. Soon bubbles started coming out of the dishwasher. There were bubbles on the dogs, bubbles on the floor. The kids were skating in the bubbles and laughing so hard they were having trouble cleaning up the mess.

Jo never let on what brats they were. If I were her, I would've decided a hundred bucks wasn't worth it, but she continued to take pity on us and continue babysitting. She has always been a terrific person, sweet and well-liked.

The kids once covered the girl's room in bubbles and jumped off the dresser to the bed. The ceiling shook in the living room and we yelled up, "What are you doing"?

"Nothing," they all said in unison as the dust fell from the ceiling fan.

One night, Marsha and I went into the den where the kids were watching the second TV. We sat on the couch and heard a crunch. There was Cap'n Crunch and Tostito chips crushed under the couch cushion. Too many just to have missed their mouths. They all denied it.

When David was on the top bunk, he cut a hole through the bottom of the mattress. Why? So, they could play "Trekkies." He was much stronger and bigger than the rest of the kids. He would grab a kid from the bottom bunk and pull her or him up, after saying "Beam me up, Scotty!" All the kids participated, so I couldn't blame them all.

One time, Daniel cried out in the middle of the night. Marsha found him under his bed. She pulled him out and he grabbed her around the neck and hugged her tightly. He said, "I'm afraid David will fall through the mattress and squish me."

"David won't fall through," she reassured him.

Then, as she was putting Daniel to bed, she looked up and saw the hole in the mattress. She took Daniel to our room to sleep. The next day we bought a very thin mattress for twenty dollars, so if they decided to do it again, it wouldn't be too much of a loss.

Once when David was messing around and wrestling on the top bunk, he scratched himself quite badly. I didn't have a bandage big enough, so I took a sanitary pad and taped it on well so he wouldn't lose it at school. Luckily there were no incidents and he was none the wiser.

*   *   *

David rarely slept, and he had a weird sense of humor that only his friends understood. His favorite number was pi: 3.141592 ad infinitum.

One night we walked into the house to find an air compressor in the living room. There were balloons filled with shaving cream all over the place, and some serious fireworks in the corner. You could tell David was home from the navy. He'd gone to Indiana to buy the fireworks, and once the guy had seen his military ID, he'd said, "Come back here and look." Needless to say, David found some pretty heavy-duty fireworks in the back room.

We saw him back in the kitchen and he asked us, "Which would fly farther, a Bundt cake or a layer cake?" It was obviously a boy party. He had built rocket launchers because he felt the cakes would fly better out of beer bottles. He was quite resourceful that way.

At Christmas one year, David made 360 loaves of pumpkin bread. He didn't really have any money because he'd just come home from the US Naval Academy, so he decided to give all those loaves of pumpkin bread to everybody he saw.

David came to us and said, "Do you know that your stove shuts off after twelve hours as a safety feature? I was right in the middle of baking my bread!"

"Nope, I didn't know our oven had that feature, because I've never tried cooking for twenty-four hours straight."

To this day we still can't stand the smell of a pumpkin candle in our house.

CHAPTER 31

Brandy

Brandy was four-foot-eleven and she had a friend who was six-one. One day I saw some kids smoking in a group at the Parish Hall. There was a tall kid and a short one. I whipped my car around and shone my headlights on them but saw it was not Brandy and her friend. So, I opened the door and said, "Has anybody here seen a little sheltie collie? No? Nobody? Okay, thank you." Boy, were those kids relieved.

Brandy took swimming lessons. When Marsha came to get her one morning, she was not in the pool. Marsha asked the lifeguard, "Why is she not in the pool?"

The lifeguard said, "She didn't want to go in because she said it was too cold."

Marsha replied, "If I was worried about her comfort, I wouldn't have put her in the first session, first thing in the morning. I paid twenty dollars for you to get her in the pool."

When Marsha came back the next morning, there was Brandy in the pool, clinging to the side, a lovely shade of purplish-blue.

Brandy went back the next year but still didn't make it through beginning swimming. She finally made it through when her younger sister Amanda did. I wanted all my kids to take swimming because I was a terrible swimmer and knew I wouldn't be able to save them if we were ever in a boat that capsized. Granted, we've never been together in a capsized boat—or any boat, for that matter—but in my head, I felt that surely someday we would be, and it would capsize, and they'd have to save themselves.

Brandy had very long, curly hair. When she was in eighth grade, just before she graduated, she decided she had to have a spiral perm. She looked like Cousin Itt from The Addams Family. We had her graduation gown pressed and hanging in the closet. She had to be there early, so she grabbed the gown and threw it over her arm and left.

Next time we saw her, her hair was a foot wide and her gown was dragging on the ground. She'd obviously grabbed her brother's from his graduation the previous year instead of hers.

Brandy can argue like a politician. One time when she was in third grade, a garbage truck was trying to get through and she stood with her hands on her hips, all four feet of her standing in front the garbage truck, refusing to let it pass. For this little feat she received a detention. The worst part: She served her first, and only, detention with David.

When Brandy was in high school, she decided she didn't want to participate in gym. So, she told the teacher she left her gym suit at home. She "left it at home" for two weeks, and then "confessed" we didn't have money for a gym suit.

The teacher called me and said, "If you can't afford a gym suit, I'll be glad to pay for it for you."

I said, "What?! Brandy has a gym suit. She just doesn't want to wear it or participate in PE." The next day, Brandy was wearing her gym suit in gym class.

Brandy had a teacher who was religious. She decided to bother the teacher by saying she was going to start a cult. She also did a paper on Wiccan. She told Amanda and Daniel there was a haunted painting in the hallway upstairs. She made a little man out of gray and black construction paper. She kept moving the man in the picture, making Amanda and Daniel afraid to go upstairs alone.

It didn't help that Marsha had a picture of the flying monkeys from The Wizard of Oz on the attic door, telling them flying monkeys were inside. The attic was unsafe, so she didn't want the kids in there. They never went in because even though they didn't believe in flying monkeys, they thought there just might be some in the attic.

CHAPTER 32

Daniel

Daniel always had a queasy stomach. Once when he was in kindergarten, the school called and told us Daniel had vomited and needed to be picked up.

Marsha went to pick him up. As he was getting into the car she opened the back door and Daniel leaned over and puked all over the back floorboard instead of the gravel parking lot. When she got him home, we gave him a bucket in case he threw up again. The next time he threw up, he moved the bucket and vomited on the couch. I guess he thought the bucket would prevent him from throwing up properly.

Our friend Vicki would come over with her son Cliff on weekends. She lived in Streator, twenty miles away. We were a stable but poor family, so Vicki often brought pizza with her. The kids would go to the pool and eat together, and Vicki and Cliff would stay the night.

One night when Vicki was visiting, Daniel threw up. The girls came to Vicki's bedroom door and rapped on it, saying, "Daniel threw up."

Vicki said, "Next door," so they went to Marsha's door.

Marsha said, "Go tell your mom."

The girls were sitting outside my door so I could hear their whole conversation.

"What'd he throw up?" Brandy asked.

Amanda replied, "Fruit cocktail."

"How do you know?"

"I saw a cherry."

Brandy asked, "Was it chewed or was it whole?"

"It was whole, but I think I saw teeth marks," Amanda said.

I was awake now, so I went to clean up the puke. It was indeed fruit cocktail, and there was a chewed cherry.

The girls told me that he'd also thrown up on Big Bear. Big Bear was a huge stuffed animal about half the size of the girls.

"Go put Big Bear in the wash," I said.

I came downstairs the next morning and saw Big Bear sitting in the washing machine with his head and arms sticking out. Ready to be washed. Somehow, Big Bear ran away and we couldn't find him anymore.

Once the kids put toothpaste on the upstairs carpeting. They saw it was a problem and put a paper towel over it.

A few days later Marsha found it. She yelled at them, "Who did this? Don't you know toothpaste sticks like concrete?!" Of course, nobody did it.

The next week the girls were in the bathtub and it overflowed. Some floor tiles lifted, and we caught them fixing the tiles with their toothbrushes and toothpaste. Remember, "Toothpaste sticks like concrete."

*　　　　*　　　　*

When Daniel was in kindergarten, he was told to wear his best outfit for the school program. He wore his baseball uniform. We were so thrilled after seeing the rest of the kids dressed to the nines and our son in a baseball uniform.

Once Daniel came home from school and said he needed more pencils. We had already given him seven, so went to the school to find out why he was losing pencils. We went to look in his desk and there were seven pencils, chewed down so he couldn't write with them. We took him over to the pencil sharpener. It was like magic! The pencils were sharpened. He smiled and asked, "Can anyone do that?" We assured him he'd be able to sharpen his pencils whenever he needed to—he just had to ask the teacher. We made sure he could do it before we left.

*　　*　　*

Daniel had little difficulty in junior high and high school. He'd seen the other kids get in trouble for everything, so he didn't try anything new. He went out one night and thought he wouldn't get caught. But our bedroom door opened and in came Murphy, the border collie. Murphy stayed downstairs at night and only came up when someone left the door open. We both knew "a kid was out." We went downstairs and noticed it had snowed a little and there were only footprints coming into the house.

At breakfast, Marsha asked, "So, who was out last night?"

No one volunteered info.

Let the interrogation begin.

"Okay, small shoeprints, so that rules out David."

Daniel looked down as Marsha said, "So Daniel, where'd you go?"

He kept looking down as he said, "To play cards with my friends."

"What did you play?"

"Euchre," he said, naming a card game popular in the Midwest.

"Okay, you can stay downstairs and clean with me," Marsha said, "starting with the baseboards."

Daniel probably didn't care, as he got to be with Marsha.

*　　*　　*

Daniel was known for not eating vegetables. It was a fight almost every night, as some kids liked corn and others liked only green beans.

Once, going through McDonald's, I asked him what he wanted.

"Not green beans or broccoli."

"They don't have vegetables here," I said.

He was relieved, and then elated when he received French fries.

CHAPTER 33

Vacations

One year we went to House on the Rock, a tourist attraction in Wisconsin. An architectural mystery with calliopes, cave-like rooms, shops, and so forth, kids twelve and under got in free.

Brandy was very tiny for her age. Marsha said everyone but David was underage, even though Brandy was thirteen.

Brandy yelled, "No, Marsha, I'm thirteen now!"

Marsha came over and said, "You're however old I say you are." So, she got in free because the attendant didn't hear Brandy's comment.

First stop after driving a long way was the restroom. The boys were scared because "there was a man in the bathroom trying to sell them stuff."

I went in to look. It was the bathroom attendant. The other men in there were surprised to see a woman talking to the bathroom attendant, saying "I just want to make sure there are no weirdos in here." If you're a woman in the men's bathroom, then you are the weirdo.

Another time we went to the Wisconsin Dells, a cool water park with other attractions. The kids all went on the rides while I lay under a blanket. I was thinking that I paid twenty bucks to get in, and that I should do something. Then I thought, The heck with it. I would pay twenty bucks for a nap.

So that's what I did.

Over the years Marsha and I took several cruises offered by Olivia Travel, a cruise company entirely for lesbians. We got picketed once in the Bahamas, so we started singing "Kumbaya." They called us sissies. We thought, "No, sissies walk on runways while we build them." A police car escorted us to a private island.

We had a blast. It was my first experience seeing a shirtless woman, and I couldn't help staring at her. Not at her boobs, but simply admiring her courage and comfort in her own body.

*   *   *

One evening Mom had no one to go out with, so she asked Ron and me to go with her.

We drove to Morris to the Holiday Inn bar. Ron and I danced while Mom drank. It was going well until we sat down.

Mom said, "You know I love you?"

"Mom, I don't want to get in a fight with you, but you only say that when you are drunk," I replied.

"I'm not drunk," she slurred.

"Okay," I said. "Whatever."

"I need to talk to you about something." She spit when she talked and lit another cigarette.

Okay, here it comes, I thought.

"Why do you live with Marsha? She seems to be a bad influence on you. You look at her like there is something more there. Like you are in love with her. You know God abhors homosexuals?"

"He also doesn't believe in divorce, adultery, public drunkenness, and judgment," I said tersely.

"Now, don't start with me. This is about you. Also, Jesus drank wine."

"Yes, but Jesus was not falling-down drunk. Also, water was not potable. They didn't have the sanitation we have now."

"Don't challenge me. This is about your relationship with Marsha. I didn't raise you this way. You were so pretty when you were thin. You don't even try to lose weight. I bet you weigh two hundred pounds now. You cut your long hair when you met her."

"I cut my hair when I was in high school, after I had a baby," I said. "You never said anything then. I grew it out because my husband liked it. I cut it off to spite him. Besides that, my relationship with Marsha is none of your business."

"I can have Donny take your children," Mom said, "and then I can babysit them or see them whenever I want. I bet he'd even let me drive them places. You better watch what you do and how you act with me. I have a lot of power you don't even know about."

"Just like always, you take sides against me," I said. "I think I'll just go home."

I left and started walking. I was twenty-two miles from Dwight, and it was cold. I had planned on being in a warm car and hadn't taken a jacket. I walked across Route 47 to a restaurant called R's Place, to call Marsha to come get me.

My brother pulled up next to me at the pay phone and rolled down the driver's-side window while Mom looked out the passenger window.

"Get in, Emory," Ron said.

"No. I'm sick of her attitude toward me. She's always hated me! I've done everything I can do to make her love me, or even like me. She never does!"

"Just get in. You don't have to talk to her or even look at her—just get in."

I hung up the pay phone and got in behind my brother. I never said a word the whole way home. I had him drop me off and take Mom with him.

They went to another bar. When my dad called a few hours later, asking what time they had dropped me off, I hesitated before lying to him.

"About fifteen minutes ago," I said.

I don't know why I lied. Maybe I was too codependent to her narcissistic personality. I had been put down, lied to, and entangled in her web for so long, I couldn't break free. Where did she begin and where did I end? She had pitted her kids against each other. For example, she had told my sister Rachael that she had bought all of my furniture. It was a total lie. We kids were jealous of each other and competed for Mom's morsels of attention.

Ron would come over from his house and I'd come from mine. Bindy lived with her. We'd all sit around her kitchen table while she held court. She'd drink her coffee and smoke her cigarettes and we'd all let Mom expound. Her self-importance knew no bounds. Looking back, I think she was secretly ashamed of her poor West Virginia upbringing and lack of education, and tried to compensate with this behavior.

CHAPTER 34

Adventures in Dieting

I have tried all kinds of weight loss programs over the years. I was up to my all-time high of 230 pounds in 2010. I had tried Weight Watchers, Seattle Sutton, Herbalife, MediQuick, Atkins, South Beach, low-carb, low-fat, high-protein, and many more. I talked to my primary doctor and I was set up for bariatric surgery. I jumped through all the hoops and was finally scheduled for surgery on a Monday.

I had been going to the gym and trying to lose weight prior to surgery. I went to my primary doctor on the Friday before surgery for a final check. This was 2005. When I got on the scale, it read 170 pounds! I was amazed and decided to cancel my upcoming bariatric surgery.

In 2015 I am back up to 200 pounds. I blame it on my meds, mostly Prednisone, which I take for Rheumatoid arthritis. But meds don't make you gain weight; your hand and fork do.

So, I keep plugging along.

*   *   *

When I decided to go to nursing school, I had to take remedial math and English. I did poorly in high school and had no study skills. I had to take a year of general education and extra science classes. School was hard for me, especially math. Also, when I took physiology the teacher was from another country and it was difficult to understand him.

The last semester, many of us had the professor who was known for having many of her students flunk her classes. We had to write care plans for patients. It was difficult. I didn't have a computer, so I handwrote a care plan eighty pages long. Luckily, she took a shine to me and I passed. My graduation came down to the test in this professor's class. In order to pass all of your nursing classes, you couldn't get a grade below 74. I received an 82. Because she was such a difficult teacher and I'd had her for sixteen weeks, I was well prepared and flew through the nursing boards with flying colors. I had worked my butt off to get through school, and after three long years, I was a registered nurse. When all was said and done, I ended up with eight years of college. I had an RN, a BSN, and an MBA.

I was the only one in my family to graduate from college. It opened many doors for me. One of those doors was at the University of St. Francis in Joliet, Illinois, where I worked to set up online programs for RNs to get their bachelor's degrees. I flew to many other states and spoke to nursing boards and departments of education to get recognized in those states. There are many online degrees available now, but we were one of the first in this area.

I had an assistant to help me. Her name was Caryn, and she took a lot of stress off me. She was as loyal and honest as anyone I've ever met. We've remained friends to this day. My secretary, Geri, saved my butt on more than one occasion. She was prompt and could handle most of the calls that came in to the office. She could walk into any Chicago office and work as an executive secretary. I was so lucky to have her.

*　　*　　*

Marsha attended a seminar to learn how to decorate with fruit and vegetables. Whenever we would have parties she always produced unusual treats. My kids knew I couldn't cook, so I always made the "relish tray," filling each section with different varieties of M&M's. My way of cooking was a hit.

CHAPTER 35

Emergency Room Nurse

I worked at two emergency rooms over the years. I loved working the ER and learned a lot. It gave me the same adrenaline rush as working for the volunteer ambulance service. The difference was, a physician was there at all times. The reason I left the ER was because I was afraid of the radio. Ambulance crews would call in on the radio and the nurses would provide directions for further treatment. Even though I had taken the appropriate classes, I wasn't confident in my radio skills. I was great with regular and trauma patients.

I had a lady who came in once, crying and speaking in Spanish as she threw her baby at me. I looked at the baby and it was blue. I assessed the baby for choking and decided to do the baby Heimlich maneuver. Out came a pacifier tip! We instructed the family through a Spanish interpreter, not to use a broken pacifier and they shook their heads in understanding. I'm not sure if they got it, but they seemed to.

Another time, a three-year-old came in with the ambulance. She had drowned in the river. We worked on her for quite a while before time was called and she was pronounced dead.

When someone dies in the ER, you need to get the body and the room ready for family to identify and view the body. You clean the floor of papers, blood, and caps of needles. IVs are removed, and a body bag is placed under the deceased, and they are covered up to their face.

Often people lose control of their bowels and bladder from the relaxation of muscles at the time of death. That was the case with this drowning victim. When I rolled the child over to clean her, blood and river water came out of her nose and mouth. It startled me, and I jumped back and quickly grabbed a towel. When I had prepared her body, I had her father come in. When asked where the mother was, he said, "She is in the maternity ward upstairs. She had a baby yesterday."

They were called and the mom was brought to the ER in a wheelchair. It was all very sad. I asked if I could accompany the body to the morgue. No one protested.

When I got to the morgue, they were doing an autopsy on a male body. I told them it wouldn't bother me. I looked at the body and saw the skin peeled back from his face. How interesting, I thought. I was fascinated. That's how people look without their skin. I soaked up new experiences like a sponge.

CHAPTER 36

Prison Nurse

After working in the ER, I took a new job as director of nursing at a nearby prison.

One of my responsibilities was to read and answer inmate requests. Mostly they wrote to request a bottom bunk, which required a physician's order. Very few qualified.

They also wrote to request tennis shoes. The state boots they were issued were uncomfortable, and many wanted something easier on the feet.

Some of them had TVs. In my opinion, they lived better than half of America. Except for the fear plaguing every inmate.

I met some famous serial killers and a lot more inmates who had committed lesser crimes. I had to admit I was a little afraid. But you never forget you are in a max prison.

In 2011, capital punishment in Illinois was abolished. I stood outside a prison when John Wayne Gacy was executed. He killed, tortured, and sexually assaulted thirty-three young men and boys. I also saw Richard Speck die at Silver Cross Hospital in Joliet. He killed eight nurses, so it was kind of ironic that nurses were the ones trying to save his life after he'd had a heart attack.

Murderer Henry Brisbon assaulted John Wayne Gacy and killed an inmate in Statesville Prison in Joliet. Henry Brisbon was facing 1,000 to 3,000 years, and was moved to death row at Pontiac Correctional Center. Ultimately, he died in prison.

They had gangs that walked in groups. You weren't supposed to cross a gang line no matter if it was an emergency or not. There are certain rules within the gang; they have their own "constitutions." There are various jobs within the gang, and each gang has various levels—generals, lieutenants, soldiers, etc. Gangs communicate in many ways, but they don't talk about their "politics." Most gangs congregate by race or the area where they're from: Bloods, Crips, Latin Kings, Aryan Brotherhood, Vice Lords, Gangster Disciples, and many more. They send letters called "kites," writing in code to make it more difficult for others to decipher.

Although Security would never admit it out loud, gangs run the prisons, often controlling the work and cell assignments. Gang members hide weapons in their clothes or on their bodies, and in various parts of their cells or around the prison. The knife-like weapons are called "shanks" or "shivs." Other weapons include batteries or a padlock in a sock; they can be real weapons made from a tool from the shop, or a homemade type constructed from things like a toothbrush or a hairbrush.

There are certain rules gang members follow to try and keep themselves "clean":

1. Don't disrespect anyone.
2. Don't ask anyone their crime. (Everybody is innocent in prison.)
3. Don't get too close to the guards or you will be considered a snitch.
4. This seems obvious, but don't have sex with the guards.
5. Make sure you have family or friends on the outside so they can send money to your account.
6. If you were in a gang on the street, you will be expected to be in the same gang inside.
7. Mind your own business and "do your own time."
8. If your gang sets out to start a fight, even if you know you're going to lose and get hurt or killed, you must fight with and for your gang—or else even your own gang will hurt or kill you.

The second time I worked there, the inmates were locked in their cells. The gangs were still in control and violence continued though not as much.

One time an inmate attacked a radiology tech and she wrote him up. He threatened her, saying that outside the prison, people would come after her. Ultimately, she committed suicide. I tried not to be prejudiced against the guy, but it was difficult.

Once the internal affairs office called me in. I was nervous. When I got there the internal affairs guy was sitting with three officers, shooting the breeze. They all looked at me and the three officers left the room. The investigator showed me some syringes and asked if they came from the hospital. I told him we have that kind of syringe, but it is usually used for insulin. He asked if I knew anything about it. I said, "No." He said, "Okay. I'll continue to investigate how these got into the cell house."

Ultimately, they found it was a guard who had brought them in. He was fired and charged.

One time, the segregation unit was on fire. I hid behind an air-conditioning unit with my keys down my bra and a radio in my pants. I decided then that I was a mom with four children and I didn't need this kind of stress. I won a medal for it, but it wasn't worth it.

It wasn't all bad; it was a good job with good pay and benefits for people who did not have a college degree. However, it does take an emotional toll, which leaks into family life. I became more irritable and sarcastic and I cussed a lot. Prison jobs often result in high divorce rates and affairs. A prison guard I talked to agreed with me. The worst thing this guard saw was an inmate who wanted to get out of the gangs. The gang beat him almost to the point of death; his face was so swollen you couldn't see his eyes.

This job led to terrible migraines for me, and as a result I called off a lot. When I broke my shoulder, I told the boss I needed to take at least two weeks off and then I could come back in. The policy was no slings or splints; you had to be fully recovered before you could come back. She said if I took time off for my shoulder I would be fired. I resigned because I didn't want to work for a company like that.

*   *   *

About five years later I took a job working for the State of Illinois, Department of mental health and developmental disabilities, but nothing had changed since I left. As an RN, there was still a lot of mandatory overtime. Sometimes I'd work as much as seventy hours per week. I had good friends there: three care-plan coordinators, Earline, Margaret, and Janet; and many RN friends, including LeeAnn, Pam, Max, and Mary Ann. I loved the housekeeper for my unit, Mary Jo. Although I loved these people, it was not enough to make me stay. I quit again. I couldn't stand the overtime, as it caused me to have migraines.

My migraines caused me to miss a lot of work. They were terrible and sent me to bed in a cold dark room. Once I had one that lasted six weeks. After that I was referred to a neurologist and started Botox treatment, which was meant to alleviate the pain. I did this for three years, and it helped some, but not enough. I was on five medications and I'd still wake up with a headache every day, albeit not always a migraine. I applied for disability for my mental health issues and my debilitating migraines. I got it on the first try, with no lawyer, which people tell me is unusual.

Later I was sent to Guardian Headache and Pain Management Institute in Bloomington. The doctor there gave me injections, which were partially effective. Then he cauterized the nerves in my neck. For three months I had no headaches. They slowly crept back, but far fewer than before.

I'm still undergoing treatment there today. An MRI was ordered and I was referred to a neurosurgeon, who said I didn't need surgery despite the fact that I had herniated discs, partially pressing on my spinal cord. I am going to get a second opinion.

CHAPTER 37

Dogs

Every September, our town has what is called Harvest Days. It's a yearly festival with crafts, flea markets, car shows, and a carnival. My brother Ron was an auxiliary police officer. One year he saw Marsha and me sitting on the curb. We waved and he turned his head and walked away. He was embarrassed by me. I was still the talk of the town. He was a proud man and didn't want to be disgraced by me. I was really hurt.

My church, New Life Assembly of God, offers free carnival games at Harvest Days for kids who are third graders and younger. It gives the parents something to do that isn't expensive during the festival. We also have a big parade on the last day, Sunday. It starts with a thousand basset hounds waddling down the street. Basset hounds tire easily. The first year the dogs were followed by the vet in a golf cart. He would scoop up the hounds that got tired as he went by. The next year he rode in a flatbed trailer to pick them all up.

*   *   *

The vet was concerned when our dog Murphy got fat He told us to get her to lose twenty pounds. When she went back for her next visit, she weighed ten pounds more.

Marsha found out all the kids had been secretly feeding her. They felt sorry for her and each gave her treats on the sly. Marsha put the dog in front of them and said, "You are going to kill your dog if you keep feeding her like this." So the kids took her for walks every day and hardly gave her any food. She was so hungry she tried to intercept the remote when it was thrown because she thought it was food.

By the next visit to the vet, she had lost twenty pounds, plus the ten she'd gained. The vet was amazed, as he had never seen a dog lose that much weight. We were all so proud.

We also had a rescue dog named Sadie, a small Sheltie (think, tiny Lassie). She decided she wouldn't be kept in the utility room, and would jump the baby gate even without a running start. She also jumped out the window. Two little girls found her after one escape and called our number, printed on her collar. We went to pick her up. The next time she escaped she came home smiling in the back of a police car.

Sadie wouldn't sleep away from Marsha. She slept on Marsha's head, all curled up like a cat. She also walked on the back of the couch like a cat. She only fell once and came out from behind the couch, looking embarrassed.

Marsha made cupcakes for me to take for a bake sale. We went to school to pick up the kids, and when we got home, I heard Marsha shout "Holy crap! Who ate all the cupcakes?!"

"Not me; I was with you," I said. "And not the kids—they were in school.

"Yet somehow it appears all twenty-four cupcakes were eaten, even the sparkly holders," said Marsha.

We saw Murphy under the table, looking guilty. She got several "Bad dogs" for it. We called puppy poison control, as the cupcakes were chocolate. For a week Murphy was shitting sparkly stuff.

The next call to puppy poison control was because Murphy ate a yellow glow stick. You could see where she'd pooped by the yellow glow in the grass. It didn't seem to affect her appetite.

One day when we'd gone to Dairy Queen, the washer overflowed. We came home and the dogs were up to their knees in water, looking guilty. They were licking up the mess, afraid they would be in trouble.

Murphy loved Dairy Queen and learned to sit in the back-seat, leaning forward to eat a small cone that I held from the driver's seat. I don't know whether or not dogs should have ice-cream cones, but it never seemed to bother her.

One time I saw Daniel and Murphy barking as people passed by. Daniel also decided he liked the cheesy dog food better than the hard stuff.

Once when Marsha was still married, the kids saw wrapped cookies in Uncle Steve's van and asked if they could have some. He obliged.

When I came back to the car, they told me, "Uncle Steve's cookies were stale." I looked around for the wrappers.

Steve was laughing when I asked, "Where are the cookies?"

He pointed to the dog treats on the front dash of his van.

That was the last time he was left alone with the kids.

CHAPTER 38

Disney

One year we saved enough money to go to Disneyworld in Florida. We got twelve miles down the road before someone farted and they all started arguing about window seats.

Marsha stopped the car and yelled, "I'm paying four thousand effing dollars for this vacation! You will not fight or argue this whole trip or you will stay in the hotel room and not go to Disney with the rest of us. If we are taking a picture, you will smile when I tell you to smile." Result: several pictures of the kids with fake smiles on their faces.

Daniel bought a Goofy hat as his gift at Disney and wore it everywhere. We took a cab to return to our car and when we got out, Goofy was left behind. Much crying ensued. We finally called the taxicab office to have them check the backs of their taxis. We paid cab fare for the Goofy hat and left a generous tip. All in all, that hat cost me seventy-five bucks, but it was worth it to see Goofy in my rearview mirror all the way from Florida to Illinois. I couldn't see Daniel, just Goofy; it was adorable. Of course, I drove home wearing my Mickey Mouse ears.

Daniel was known for getting caught for everything he did. One day the school called asking why Daniel had rope marks on his neck. I replied that I didn't know but would speak with Daniel that night. Turns out Daniel had put a rope around his neck that morning with the other end tied to his bed. He then took off to see if he could break the rope.

David was watching and did not intervene. "Daniel came to an abrupt stop. His feet left the ground and went over his head."

Nice big brother.

Daniel, being the youngest, often provided comical fodder for his siblings. We colored the eggs one Easter, followed by an Easter egg hunt. We were missing one of the eggs at the end but didn't think too much about it.

Three weeks later, the egg was found by Daniel. The shell had gone soft, but when Brandy told him to try the egg, he bit into it, shell and all. Luckily, he spit it out before chewing.

Poor Daniel.

CHAPTER 39

My Family of Origin

My dad had a heart attack and was on blood thinners. He couldn't tolerate the cold. So, they moved to North Carolina to be near mom's brother. My sister Roxy moved with them as she was only fourteen in 1984. They would come from North Carolina for visits at my house. For one visit Marsha made twenty-seven pork chops and laid out a big buffet. My whole family, fifteen in all, got up and left us with the dishes. They went over to my Aunt Bindy's, who lived in a trailer a few blocks away. She had her own place since Mom and Dad moved. A few hours later they all went out to have pizza and beer and didn't invite me. I felt hurt, like I'd felt during many a holiday when my mom hadn't included me, or when she'd told the relatives I wasn't a real member of the family. I would not enable her. She didn't like that.

My mom came home from the pizza and beer and was fall-down drunk. We got into a fight because she had returned to my house so late and was drunk in front of my kids.

The next day was Christmas and my mom was passed out on the couch. I had to tell my kids they couldn't open presents yet because Mom-Maw was drunk. The kids were good and patient as I tried to get her awake enough for them to open their gifts.

"Is Mom-Maw still drunk or can we come down?" the kids called from upstairs. It was the first time my kids were aware of how drunk she was. I had kept the kids away from her because I knew what could happen when she was drunk.

We opened presents once the rest of the family arrived. My mom had had a shower by then and was drinking coffee.

David had wanted a Nintendo in the worst way that year. My mom liked David and Jeremy (Ron's first son), and had bought both of them a Nintendo. Jeremy opened his first. David was crestfallen to see Jeremy with his most desired gift. David stopped opening packages and just stared at the Nintendo, on the verge of tears.

Mom said, "Open yours, David." He was elated.

She bought clothes for Brandy and Daniel and for Amanda, a toy she wanted.

Her gifts made my coloring books, kites, and cards look chintzy. We always tried to have some extra gifts from us to compensate for the fact that my mother played favorites. If your name wasn't Jeremy, David, or Amanda, you didn't count to her. She would buy expensive gifts for others at times, but it was usually not what they wanted. One time Daniel got a piggy bank shaped like a log and I got a castle. I didn't get it.

I think she was continuing the pattern she'd established with her own kids. She adored Ronny and Roxy but forgot about me and Rachael. She loved our cousins, JoJo and Thad, who were raised as our siblings. I wondered why I wasn't ever good enough.

The only thing she did with me was play Scrabble. I was her toughest opponent from a young age. I really treasured those times. She had a very expensive Scrabble game that rotated and had gold letters. After she died, the Scrabble game went to Ron. I was crushed, as those were the only special moments I'd ever had with her. She left me an expensive necklace, although I didn't tend to wear much jewelry. I later pawned it because we needed extra money to make a house payment.

I don't know if she specified these legacies in her will or if she'd verbally told Roxy of her wishes. Roxy lived two blocks from her and saw her daily. Roxy told me later that our mom had stopped drugging and drinking when she'd gone to law school. I would have liked to believe that, but it's not what I saw when she came to my house. Her drug use may have lessened, but she still went out drinking with Alice.

Once I was watching a bunch of the kids and Mom and her friend Donna came home drunk. I hid eight kids and my nephew upstairs and told them to stay in the room and lock the door. I heard a lot of screaming.

I went downstairs to see them punching each other on the floor over something important: an area code and phone number. Donna lived in Chicago and was too drunk to realize you had to dial 312, as we had the 815 area code. At that time, we didn't even need to dial the area code if we were within its area. We just dialed 584 and four additional numbers.

That night I got rid of Donna by calling her ex in Chicago. He was thrilled to drive the eighty-nine miles at four a.m.

I yelled at my mother and she went to sleep in her car. I took her a blanket and a cup of coffee and her constant companion, cigarettes. She had the doors locked so I left the blanket and cigarettes on the hood.

About three days later I found her on the ground, drunk in the backyard. My brother Ron helped me get her in the house.

Despite all the drugs and alcohol, she was still classy and pretty when she was sober.

My mom had completed her undergrad degree and was now going to law school in North Carolina. She had never finished high school, so I was very proud when she went on to be a lawyer. The problem was, she never charged much and never made enough money to accommodate her champagne tastes. She also didn't pay taxes. By that time my dad had had a heart attack and couldn't work; he couldn't bring in the money he had before. Nonetheless, my mom never changed her spending habits.

*   *   *

We decided to go to North Carolina for Thanksgiving one year. My mom had other guests coming for dinner, but when we got there at 9:00 a.m., my mom had done nothing but thaw the turkey. Marsha had had an hour of sleep, but I went to her and told her the situation: We had twenty people coming and nothing was even started. Thus, I became sous chef to Marsha's chef.

We sent my dad, who had dementia, to the store with Brandy—possibly not the best choice, as they got lost. Brandy had no sense of direction, as she didn't drive, and she was too shy to talk to anyone. My dad couldn't remember words at this point. Dad finally called, and I sent my uncle to go get them. They followed my uncle home and Marsha and I quickly made the meal.

My mother sat there saying "I don't know what it feels like to sit and do nothing."

Yeah, right, I thought.

I could count every meal she'd ever made at the holidays on one hand. Mostly she sat at the table and smoked and drank while everyone else did the work. Even at Christmas the kids couldn't have a drink of her eggnog because it was spiked.

Good mother, huh?

CHAPTER 40

Broken House

We had a realtor friend named Tim Soal who came to look at the house. We were behind on our payments and knew we couldn't make them anymore. Our house had so many issues. We asked him what he thought.

"You'd have to fix all the problems," he said.

"Like the sink that pours water on your feet when you do the dishes?" I said. "And the illegal sewer trap that overflows even with a small rain, so we have to clean it out with a coat hanger? Or maybe the water heater that Marsha goes down to light in just her bra and underwear? She always says if it blows up, she doesn't want to dirty her good clothes by falling in the mud down there."

Bill advised us to just do a "deed in lieu," which means you can walk away but lose your equity and your credit. "Your credit already sucks, so that won't matter," he said.

"We can do that?" I asked incredulously. "We can just walk away?"

He nodded.

So that's what we did. It was easy and the bank was nice. Three months after getting that new toilet, we moved.

*   *   *

Our old house had six bedrooms, and we were overwhelmed when it came time to move. David carried lots of stuff out of the house and burned it, while good friends from church, Tina and her parents, Larry and Loretta, helped us pack up boxes in preparation to move. Tina, who should have been an event planner she was so organized, set up a calendar at church for volunteers to assist us, advising them to bring a sack lunch. Twenty-five people showed up on moving day. Not only did they move us to our new condo, but they also put away all our stuff and broke down the empty boxes. After eight hours, we were done!

We could never thank them enough. Our church is made up of true Christians, and they are always a godsend, over and over again. When we were sick, they brought us a week's worth of meals. A pretty high school girl from church named Bethany came and vacuumed and mopped the house. When I had to have surgery, she came and washed my hair, as I couldn't lift my arms over my head.

*   *   *

After living in the blue house on Old Route 66 for about forty years, all told, I thought I would miss it more than I did. After all, it was my childhood home.

I tried to think about it logically. This house had so many memories, but a lot of bad things had happened in that house. I tried to make it a home for Marsha and my kids, to make happy memories, and there were some. But overall the house was depressing for me. The living room was dark, with north and west windows. No matter how we decorated it, moving furniture, painting, changing accessories, it never took away the shame and pain. I was very depressed in this house. I offered it to all my siblings when we moved, but no one wanted it.

Our new condo had lots of light. It was cozy and easy to keep clean. I only have good memories at the new place. I think I would have died if I'd stayed any longer at the old house on Route 66.

Marsha and I lived alone at the new condo, except for one year when David moved in. We also had grandchildren most every weekend, from the oldest to the youngest. We are very lucky to have a great landlord, Andy Kelleher. When the furnace went out in the middle of the night, I called him and he was there within minutes. Mowing, snow removal, and maintenance are always kept up. We are blessed to have him as our landlord.

CHAPTER 41

Almost Dying

I've almost died several times in my life—twice by drowning. Both of those times I'd gone into the deep end when I was young.

The first time, I was in a pool. All of a sudden, I felt myself going up and down a few times before one of my mom's boyfriends saved me. The last thing I remember was seeing my mom. The bitch had a smirk on her face.

I had blacked out and remember waking up and the guy was kissing and blowing air into my mouth. I started coughing. I looked over to my mom and she screamed at me, "What were you trying to do? You wanted to ruin my date? Now I guess he won't come back! You're an idiot!"

The second time Brad, Bernie's husband, saved me in a lake. I wasn't living with them at the time, but they had invited me to the sportsmen's club. This near drowning wasn't as impressive as the first, but I was close to death nonetheless. This is why my kids all had to take swimming lessons. To this day I'm so afraid of water I can barely shower. I'm definitely a relaxing-in-the-tub kind of girl.

I've had several pulmonary emboli over the years. The third time I almost died I had a saddle embolus covering both my lungs. I had been fatigued and lay on the couch for days. Marsha came home from a party, took one look at me, and said, "Get dressed. I'm taking you to the hospital. You can go in your T-shirt and underwear or you can get dressed."

I got dressed, saying, "Okay, we can go to supper afterwards."

I found out later that most people die of a saddle embolus within the first two hours.

When we got to the hospital we asked how big the embolus was. They said they couldn't tell me. When Marsha went and questioned them, they showed her the films, saying, "It looks like the embolism has exploded—like she's full of buckshot."

I was put into ICU. I was upset I couldn't leave because I sure had a taste for Chinese food. Nope, nothing but hospital food for the next few days.

I would go on to have five more blood clots over the years—one in each of my lungs, one in my neck, and two under the arm. These things all could have killed me, but didn't.

*   *   *

After all of my kids had moved out, in 2003, I started taking a short-term anxiety pill. This was in addition to my meds for bipolar. Although I'd suffered from depression most of my life, I'd been diagnosed with bipolar when I was thirty. I'd always been erratic and depressed, but also hyper and impulsive. I went on spending sprees even though I didn't have the money to cover it, putting it on credit cards. I had school loans, regular bills, and now credit card debt. I was remorseful after I spent the money, and this put me into a deeper depression. When I was manic, I'd go for days without sleep, talking fast like I was on coke. While I liked the mania—I could get a lot done—the depression that followed was serious.

I went to my therapist and told her how I felt depressed but also extremely anxious. I felt like my skin was on fire and I was crawling out of it. I hadn't slept for five days. I was seeing things, usually people. It was decided by my therapist that I needed to go to the hospital.

If you are determined to be a danger to yourself or anyone else, you must go to the hospital by ambulance. You can't drive yourself even if the hospital is across the street. While I waited in the ER, I tried to escape twice, and then thought some men speaking Russian nearby were going to put me behind a wall. In truth, they were doing some remodeling work and closing off the room next to me, and they really were Russian.

I had my clothes taken away and was put into a gown. Then I waited at the hospital until they could find a bed for me at a psych ward. An ambulance had to transport me. I was admitted after a physical exam and shown to a room. The sheets smelled like old people—sanitized old people, but old people nonetheless.

I could hear someone screaming down the hall. "Let me go! Let me go, you son of a bitch!"

I guessed that this would have been a bad time to ask for a sandwich.

I saw them carry the struggling girl down the hall to the "quiet room." I supposed it was to keep the other "animals" from causing a stampede.

I went back to bed and tried to sleep but was unable to because of my roommates' snoring and crying out. I folded the flat pillow in half and brushed my short sticky hair out of my ears. Sometimes when people are depressed, they don't attend to their personal hygiene.

I had enough trouble sleeping under the most perfect circumstances. In a few hours, a person in a heavy coat came for some of my roommates. They got dressed and put on their coats. I wondered where three patients and a mental health technician were going at four in the morning.

Soon, light began showing through the window. I looked at the peeling paint on the walls, noticing areas that looked like they'd been scratched by fingernails. The mirror in the bathroom was made of some kind of material that distorted your reflection. It was such a weird illusion. Most people in there had an odd sense of self anyway.

I heard a noise in the hall and smelled food.

They came and told us to get up and get ready for breakfast. In the group room I saw a few people in their pajamas sitting around the table. I examined the food. Cold eggs, sausage, toast, and yogurt. I didn't eat much. I'm a picky eater even if it's something I like. Another patient told me, "They monitor what you eat, and they count the silverware."

"What could my plastic spoon do to hurt someone?"

"It's not necessarily other people they worry about you hurting; it's yourself as well."

I found out later her name was Patty and she said she had "multiple personalities." I wasn't sure I believed in that diagnosis. I was thinking Sybil. Makes for a good movie but not real life. Of course, who was I to judge "real life"? I was a patient in a psych ward who happened to be a nurse. I was there because I was depressed. So is half the country.

What put me here?

*   *   *

I remember being at work one day and I was just so sad. I had been sad for a while. Nothing seemed to help. The mandatory overtime, the bickering, the gossip, the bullying. Suddenly I just couldn't take it anymore. I walked out, throwing my keys at the person working the front desk, not waiting to see the surprised look on the security guard's face.

I know part of it was my empty nest syndrome and my new meds. I had never been an adult without my kids. Having your first child at sixteen means you grow up with your children. Being a mother was the best thing that had ever happened to me. It meant I got away from my mother and family, but more than that, I had created a new normal with Marsha and my kids. I had the perfect family and partner. Why was I so sad?

CHAPTER 42

Meeting the Others

I was lying down on my bed when they came to tell me that I would have to attend group meetings. I didn't want to go. I was depressed, and didn't feel like talking to anyone.

I slowly walked down the hall, dragging my feet like a toddler being forced to do something he doesn't want to do. I entered the room and noticed the room was full and there were no seats facing the door. I always had to face the door. If I don't face the door, something bad will happen. Someone could sneak up on me.

I stood on the side of the room facing the door. The facilitator told me to sit down. I went to the other side of the room and pulled the chair back around so I was facing the door with my back to the wall. A girl with lots of clothes on and a tube in her nose held herself tightly, like she was covering herself with a blanket made of her own body.

Introductions were made and then we were supposed to talk. The facilitator introduced herself as Kate and then went around the room asking questions of each of us.

I sat quietly at first. But then I decided that if I were to get better, I needed to participate. The staff counted the times you went to group and monitored your participation.

I was trying to find thoughts and words when the girl next to me, Sara, started to talk to me.

"So, you're new here?" Sara said.

"Yes," I muttered.

"Why do you look so sad?" she asked.

"I don't know," I replied, and I truly didn't. No reason in the world.

"Why do you have a tube in your nose?" I asked her in return.

"They say I have an eating disorder," Sara replied. "I think I'm okay."

Patty cut in. "I was sexually abused causing me to have multiple personality disorder. I can go days to weeks without being myself. I see people I don't know but they know me. It's embarrassing. My mom and dad put me out when I was sixteen after I ran away with a band. They put out an APB on me and offered a reward. Perhaps you read about me the papers?"

"I didn't read about you. I'm not sure about multiple personalities," I said doubtfully.

"Are you calling me a liar?" she yelled. She then curled into a fetal position and began to suck her thumb.

What a show, I thought. I now believed in it less than before.

Kate broke in and said, "Everyone is here now. Let's begin. How are you doing, Jantu?"

"I don't have much to tell," Jantu said. "My fiancé will take me out of here soon and we will go to the Middle East and be married. He currently has one wife. I will be the second and we will have lots of children. I am young enough to give him many sons. He currently wants between twenty and twenty-six."

"How will you feel about wearing something that looks like a beekeeper's outfit from head to toe, with only a slit to see through?" Sara said.

"I will wear it proudly, because he doesn't want other men looking at me. I will be his most special bride," Jantu said, then adds, "My parents hate him."

Kate said, "Okay, let's move on and hear from another people. Robert, how about you? How are you doing with your rage issues?"

"Well, I've been here five days and I feel I am getting better and gaining coping skills."

Kate asked, "What happened with your wife yesterday?"

"Well, we were visiting, and she said something to piss me off. She really knows how to push my buttons."

"I saw you try to throw the chair out the window," Kate said sternly.

"Yeah, those chairs are heavy, and the window didn't break, so it must be specially treated. No harm, no foul."

"Back to your wife," Kate said. "You know you are leaving today or tomorrow. Why didn't you try to use your coping skills?"

"I just didn't think of them. I was so mad."

"You need to have them listed on paper until you've completely memorized them. That's the way it works. When you get mad, refer to your list. That should help you from acting out. What are some of your coping skills?"

"Walk away, do an activity I enjoy, sit down and listen and talk quietly, go for a walk but not to a bar, don't drink, and take my meds. Remember, I live for my two little girls. They are now three and five. I love those kids."

"That sounds like a great start," said Kate. "How about you, Patty? Are you back with us?" Patty had removed herself from the fetal position but continued to suck her thumb.

I noticed halfway through her that Patty returned to using an old lady's voice, which made me more skeptical. A few minutes ago, she'd been saying she ran away with a band and her parents had kicked her out.

Kelly said, "I bet a lot of us here were sexually abused but no one else claims to be a multiple personality. I don't believe you." Patty began to cry and ran from the room.

Kate spoke again. "We are not here to criticize anyone or their story. We must be careful. We don't want anyone to backslide."

CHAPTER 43

Their Stories

At our next group session, Sara said, "I shouldn't be here. I don't like to talk about my life. I just want to be left alone. They say I have a disease. They make me eat and talk and share. They put me on a feeding tube because they say I have anorexia and bulimia. I really don't, but I have to stay thin because I'm an athlete. I'm good in school—at least I was when I used to go. I used to be pretty and popular, according to my mom."

Sara continued. "My parents have been freaking out. They are wealthy but I wouldn't say well-off, because that implies they are emotionally healthy, and I don't think they are. They're so fake.

"I'm always cold and have to wear several layers. They made me take them off to be weighed when I got here. I am five-six and I weigh eighty-two pounds. I 'should' weigh a hundred and thirty to a hundred and forty pounds—so say the charts. I wear a hat. I have lost almost all of my hair. It comes out in handfuls. My teeth look terrible from all the vomiting.

"My parents didn't notice until I was twelve that I had stopped eating. I'm now nineteen but people think I'm younger because I look like a child. I needed to lose weight from the point of view of my running coach. I skipped meals and exercised. My coach said I needed to lose weight more quickly, so I started portioning the little food I did eat. I felt guilty about the small amounts I ate. I checked my weight about ten to fifteen times per day. I increased my exercise because I was still fat. I weighed a hundred and five pounds then.

"My parents started noticing I was getting thin. They didn't say too thin, so I kept exercising. I was working toward 'too thin.' When I was ninety pounds my mother asked me why I always wore layers and layers of clothing. 'It makes you look dumpy and fat.' I took that to mean that I was dumpy and fat. Truth was, I wore all of those clothes to disguise my weight loss. Plus, the more weight I lost, the paler and more anemic I became."

Sara paused for a moment, then went on.

"I was in the shower one day and my mother came in to do her makeup. She was wearing her black Halston dress with a diamond necklace my father got her for Christmas. She had her bleached blonde hair pulled back with an antique comb, and she carried a Gucci purse. She looked exquisite.

"She saw me drying off and stood there, openmouthed and horrified. She said, 'Oh my God, you're so thin! You look like a concentration camp survivor! How could you do this to me? Now we need to go to the hospital, and I'll have to miss the party tonight.' She looked at her watch and said, 'If we leave right now, I can drop you off and still make the party. I'll tell your father later tonight.'

"Then she brought me here. She walked me into the hospital, filled out the insurance forms, and said, 'She is too thin—she needs help. You need to admit her. I will call back later to check on her.'

"The secretary said, 'I'm sorry, but to be admitted here she needs to want to hurt herself or someone else. Does she feel that way?' I thought, 'No, I want to improve myself by being thinner. It's all right for popular girls, but not for me?'

"My mom never skipped a beat. She said, 'Yes, she wants to hurt herself. Can't you see her? Look, we have someplace to be. Sara, you're nineteen—you can fill out these papers.' I nodded my head because that's what I do. I'm the 'perfect daughter.'"

*　　　*　　　*

Then it was Patty's turn to speak.

"I have MPD, otherwise known as multiple personality disorder. It's usually called 'dissociative personality state' these days. I have at least three personalities: a sixty-three-year-old woman who lives alone—I'm lonely; a toddler, three years old, named Sherry; and a seventeen-year-old, pretty and fit, a homecoming queen. Her name's Katrina.

"I can't remember anything and I frequently lose time. I once found myself at the train station with a suitcase full of teenage clothing and a guitar with a hundred dollars in my pocket. The clothes didn't fit, and I wondered where I'd gotten them. Some-one somewhere was missing their clothes. I turned them into the lost-and-found at the train station, thinking I had picked up the wrong bag. I kept the money. No one would miss it.

"I feel detached from myself. People around me seem 'un-real.' I have a lot of stress. I am retired and I don't have enough money to live on. I'm on disability but too young for Medicare, and with the disability I make too much mon-ey for Medicaid. So, I must buy marketplace insurance. It costs me a hundred and seventy-one dollars a month. Bills, food, and so on—how will I pay for everything?

"Sometimes I don't pay the bills on time because my other personalities are not responsible. I don't feel like 'myself,' whoever that is. I have no family or friends. I don't have hobbies. My eyes are too bad to read; I'm too deaf to listen to audiobooks.

"I have nothing and I do nothing. I am a lost cause. I'm always suicidal. That's why I'm always here."

*　　　*　　　*

Next, it was Jantu's turn.

"I am nineteen years old. I go to the University of Illinois. I am going to be a doctor and the wife of Omar bin Laden. He is the fourth son of Osama bin Laden, the head of al-Qaeda. Some say Omar is dead, but I know better. He's in hiding, waiting for me to finish college. I don't know why I'm here. They say I have delusions, that I'm an undifferentiated schizophrenic. I'm not sure what those words mean.

"I think my parents put me here because they don't want me to get married so young after college. Omar was picked by his father to be his successor. He has conflicts with his famous father, but he knows his father would never harm him. He doesn't believe in his father's ideals and beliefs. He and his family are wealthy. He is thirty-six years old and has one wife already.

"My parents are very worried that I am here. They have already arranged my marriage and it is not with Omar. I will have a big wedding in Saudi Arabia and move there. My parents want a big wedding for me here, and for me to stay in America and be a doctor. Live with a computer nerd husband, have many grandchildren and a lot of money. But how can you put a price on love? Omar and I met over the Internet six months ago.

"When I get out, I am leaving. My parents visit, but my dad questions me while my mom cries. He is full of anger. I am his 'little girl.' I've never rebelled before, so this is taking a toll on them."

*　　　*　　　*

Kelly spoke next.

"I went to a therapist and told her: I have a fast heartbeat, queasiness, apprehension—especially anxiety; I worry about everything. I am moody and I'm told I have ADD. My life is a day of what-ifs. 'What if my children get sick?' 'What if they get cancer?' 'What if they get kidnapped?' 'What if they are bullied at school?' 'What if no one likes them?' 'What if my husband leaves me?' 'What if I lose my job?' 'Am I a good mother?'

"My heart is always racing and skipping beats. Sometimes I can't breathe. 'What if I have lung cancer?' 'I have a rash down there. What if my husband cheated and gave me an STD?'

"I called my therapist and told her I was going to kill myself. I really didn't mean it. All I really want to know is, why am I here? Am I crazy?"

*   *   *

Robert was the next to share his story.

"I like sex. I like a lot of sex. I am married. My wife has sex with me only once a week. I need way more than that. Five nights a week would not be enough. She gets mad that I go elsewhere. I used to go to prostitutes. I didn't feel that was cheating. It was never the same person; I didn't get attached to anyone.

"But now I'm seriously looking at my secretary. I think that would make it 'real.' The prostitutes were just a fake fantasy. My secretary and I have been flirting constantly. I think if I asked her, she would be happy to have sex with me. But I'm not sure she would do it for the right reasons. She might think she would get a salary increase or move up in the company. She wouldn't know it's just for my pleasure.

"My wife told me that if I didn't stop, she is going to leave me. I'm afraid she will, but it's not enough to make me stop. When she told me she was leaving, we had a big fight. It got physical. I just pulled her arm back and twisted. It broke and we went to the ER. She gave them an excuse, saying that she 'fell down the stairs.' She gave me an ultimatum never to hit her again, and to stop having affairs and sexual escapades with other people. I don't know if I can do it. I can try, but I don't know.

"They say I have a sexual addiction and need anger management. I'm not sure being here will help me. I don't know if I can be fixed. I get mad easily, but it's not really a problem. So, I have a short fuse? It's just something people around me need to realize. They just need to stop being so annoying.

"I don't really like people. They all seem to have a stick up their ass or they're cheesy nerds. I am a mechanic. I make good money, but people act like they are 'better than me' because I never went to college. I learned to fight at an early age. In my neighborhood, you were the aggressor or got your ass whipped.

"I've hit my wife a couple of times because she pushes my buttons. One time I ripped her blouse open and made her have sex with me. She never wants sex. She's my wife; it's her obligation. She never stops nagging me. She goes on and on about dumbass things. She gets pissed when I watch sports and drink a few beers or when I go out with the guys. Women throw themselves at me. They think I'm a catch. I'm muscular, and I work out.

"My mother says I 'never call or come by.' But she's so boring. She talks about old people stuff. She says I don't treat my wife well. She says I need help and if I don't get it, my wife will leave me. It seems like everyone is all about Me, Me, Me. That's how it's always been. Everything I do is for my mother or my wife. I can't make everyone happy. So, why the hell am I here?"

CHAPTER 44

My Story

A few days later I attended one of my individual sessions with the doctor.

"So, Emory," the doctor said, "how are you doing?"

"I am still depressed. I feel hopeless, and helpless. I feel nothing. Only bad things, nothing good," I replied.

"Do you still feel suicidal?"

"Yes, I still think about it a lot. I feel unworthy. Why would anybody care about me?"

"When was the last time you thought about hurting yourself?"

"About five minutes ago."

"What's the longest time you've gone without thinking about hurting yourself?"

"About five minutes," I replied.

"Is there anything that makes it better?"

"Nope. If there was, don't you think I would have already done it?"

"Not necessarily. Some people just get into the depression and can't find their way back out," he said.

"I can't find my way out. I can't find my way up. I have no hope. I have no love. I have no peace. I have no friends, and my family doesn't care."

"I thought you had a very supportive relationship," the doctor said.

"I do. My relationship is great. But I feel guilty about being gay. I am religious, and biblically I think it is wrong," I said sadly.

"Don't you think God made you this way?"

"No, I guess I don't. I feel guilty and sad. I am an embarrassment to my children and I've made life more difficult for them."

"I understand you had a lot of abuse in your childhood."

"My mother never cared about any of us kids, but I was her main target."

I went on to tell him more about what I'd experienced.

The doctor sat back in his chair after listening to my story about Clyde at the farm.

"I'm so sorry that happened to you. This explains your mistrust and fear of men, as well as your fear of 'payback'—that nothing is given freely; there is always a catch. I believe you need to continue individual and group therapy, and I'd like to discuss your medications. I am putting you on one hundred milligrams each of Lamictal and lithium. That combination works well for bipolar, which is what I think you have. You have had periods of mania where you shop and spend excessively. You are impulsive and overly sexual. I believe this makes you bipolar instead of just depressed. You are going through the depressive phrase right now.

"Our session is over for today. You may go to group now. You should attend all of your sessions even if you don't feel like it. It can only help you. Everyone here wants you to get better, Emory."

I wondered how long I would have to be in the psych ward. What would I have to do to get better? I just didn't know.

CHAPTER 45

Group Sessions

I still felt crappy when I went to my group session, but I was glad for the distraction. The facilitator was talking to Robert about his issues and his release.

"How much of your anger is related to your dad's alcoholism?" Kate asked.

"In counseling I've learned it was a big part of my life," Robert said quietly. "I never learned how to be a proper husband and father. I just continued the cycle of abuse. My dad beat my mother and us kids. We never knew what set him off. It might have been his alcoholism.

"I could never have friends over when I was a kid. He'd grab me by the back of my pants and start swinging. Usually with a belt, sometimes a switch from our weeping willow trees. He'd send me out to cut it. I tried to find one that didn't have as much flexibility so it wouldn't whip around my legs. The less-bendy ones were better. He'd continue until I had welts and blood; only then would he stop.

"If my mother cried or tried to interfere, she would be next. He would grab her and throw her against the furniture, the wall, punch her, kick her, throw her on the floor. Then he would drag her into the bedroom. I'd listen to her cries and screams. When I was older, I realized he was raping her, but at the time I was just glad it wasn't my turn. I still feel very guilty about that. I'm still trying to get it all together and be a better husband and father than my dad was."

Kate said, "I'm glad you are trying to break the cycle, Robert. You are being released into your wife's care tonight. She needs to be with you constantly for the next few days. You are to use your coping skills, and be sure to attend individual, couples, and group intensive counseling every day. Also, you need to continue with your med program. This is no different than what's being asked of anyone else. You are not being punished or treated unfairly, I assure you."

"Where do I get the money for all this?" Robert asked. "I'm a mechanic. I make good money, but we have bills to hell and back. I can't miss work. I'll get fired."

Kate replied, "You can get family medical leave from work. Your insurance should cover the cost of the counseling sessions, and short-term disability should cover the rest. Different insurances cover different things."

Kate knew this might not be totally true, but she needed to allay Robert's fears.

Moments later Robert's wife appeared. She was wearing a yellow shirt with fashionable white pants and cute flowered deck shoes. With her blonde hair pulled back in a ponytail, she looked like both the girl next door and a dressed-down debutante.

She smiled at Robert and asked, "How are you, honey? Feeling better?"

You could see the concern and love in her eyes. You could also see the makeup trying to conceal a bruised cheek and swollen lip.

"Yeah, but this is going to be a big hassle, using money we don't have."

"I'll work extra hours, honey; we will be fine. We always are," she said optimistically.

Robert looked around at all of us. "I guess this is goodbye. I hope everyone gets better and goes home soon."

We all said good-bye and wished him well.

"There are papers at the desk you need to sign before you leave," Kate said. And with a smile, she added, "Good luck. We hope we don't see you again."

*   *   *

Patty burst into the room. "I just met with the doctor and he said I could go home—but I'm not ready! He said I could go to counseling somewhere else, outside of here. But I'm suicidal. How can he just let me go?"

Kate replied, "Patty, you know we only keep people for seven to ten days. We are a short-term facility. You need to learn your coping skills and use them at home. You will be leaving us after lunch."

Patty burst into tears and left the room.

After she left, I said, "I think she's just lonely and considers the staff her family. I think she's faking the whole multiple personality thing."

Other people murmured agreement with my thoughts.

I didn't want them to agree with me. I wanted them to make up their own and go from here.

*   *   *

"Okay, Sara, we haven't heard from you yet. What's going on today?"

"They are making me eat. Not only through the tube, but now orally, from the plate. I must eat whatever they serve even if I hate it. They watch me eat and they weigh me three times a day. They turn the scale around so I can't see it. They look at it and write it down before and after dinner.

"Yesterday, I had to eat pork chops and cottage cheese and apples, all of which I hate. I haven't eaten any solid food for over a year. I've only eaten pudding or applesauce and things like that. It tastes good going down and it's easy to throw up. The food they give me here is hard to throw up. They feed me then lock my door so I can't go to the bathroom to throw up. I try to walk the halls as a method of exercise. If they catch me, I am made to sit and eat more. My calories and carbs and fats are counted.

"My parents haven't called or visited since I've been here. They have better things to do, like going to parties and meetings."

I noticed she still looked very thin despite the forced feedings.

"I can see why this upsets you," said Kate. "I'm sorry. It's sad. Obviously, family counseling is in order, along with individual counseling."

"They won't do it. They don't care and they don't have time. Especially for me. For my brother, yes, but not for me."

"Why do you think your brother is so special?" Kate asked.

"My parents have always made that very clear. He went to the right school, became a surgeon and a lawyer. He married the right girl. Had the right number of children. Always the best. I try, but I can never measure up."

"We will work on this in family counseling," Kate responded sympathetically.

*　　　*　　　*

"Kelly, how about you? How are things going? I understand you have excessive anxiety. Are they helping you with this?"

Kelly, her voice weak and trembling, quickly replied. "When I came here, I was on Valium and I drank a lot. Initially it helped with the anxiety, but then it seemed to be less effective. I've lived with this for more than seven months. I think it was because I was in counseling and started to remember the abuse I suffered as a kid. Since then I have insomnia, or I sleep all day as a protective measure. I have been on edge, I'm irritable; I have poor concentration and I'm forgetful. I feel like I'm choking. I think I've improved some; I am doing relaxation techniques, deep breathing, and meditation; plus I'm taking my medication and doing cognitive behavior therapy."

Kate said, "Let me explain cognitive behavior therapy, known as CBT for short. Many of you will be doing this.

161

You will work with a therapist to see how thoughts and feelings influence behavior. Kelly, are they using exposure therapy with you?"

"Yes, they are. They have exposed me to things that worry me, making me less afraid. It's been gradual, but it seems to be working. Of course they are using regular therapy and counseling as well."

"Great," said Kate. "Keep working at it—you are doing well."

Kate announced it was time to break for lunch. We filed out of the room, looking forward to the respite it provided from our intense regimen.

CHAPTER 46

Guilt

We could talk freely in the cafeteria.

"I'll be glad when I can get rid of these paper scrubs," I said. "I'm glad they never took my silverware like they do for some people. I guess they weren't too afraid of my suicide attempts."

Sara replied, "They figure out your privileges based on all the paperwork and the naked physical you have to do when you come in. It seems weird, but it works. Only sometimes they don't tell you, and end up eating salad with your fingers."

"When will I get my clothes back?" I asked. "These scrubs are itchy and not quite my size."

Sara said, "Pretty soon. Your doctor gets to decide. It's best to be honest with him. He's a good doctor."

Patty said, "I never get silverware because I'm always suicidal. I never get out of the paper scrubs even when they let me go home, I am that bad. I was sexually abused all the time. My personality just split when it happened. I would pretend I was someone else and somewhere else, so I wouldn't feel the pain. It was a priest who abused me. I just dissociated; that means I voluntarily escaped from reality. I've had treatment with meds, psychotherapy, and CBT. Nothing works for me. When I go home after lunch, I will attempt suicide again so I can come back."

It was sad, but most everyone ignored her like the boastful kid on the playground. We basically voted her off the island.

Sara said, "Why don't you at least try and work the program instead of just coming back? You say you switch to another personality; I think you just use that as an excuse.

A lot of us were sexually abused and we don't claim to have split personalities. We take responsibility for our problems."

I said, "Look over there."

We all looked over to see Steve and Kelly's hands sliding up each other's knees. Soon the petting became a little more frantic. They got up and left the room.

Sara said, "We are on fifteen-minute checks. Hope they can get done with their business by then or there'll be hell to pay."

*   *   *

A few minutes later, Sara and I had the chance to have a deeper conversation.

"I know this is off the subject, but why do you feel guilty for being gay?" Sara asked. "It's okay, you know. You love who you love. You are a child of God. God made you and he doesn't make mistakes, gay or straight."

"Thank you for saying that," I replied. "I'm a Christian, and I've always felt guilty about being gay. I tried to be straight. I've only had consensual sex with two men. My first love, the father of my first child. I loved him and thought we would marry. But he left me. I told him afterwards that he was never to come back. I didn't want him to have anything to do with the child, or me.

"I was pregnant with my son when my future husband wanted to date me. I went out with him, but told him to stay away from me because I was trouble. I was pregnant and would only cause him complications. I think he decided then that he wanted to marry me, to rebel against his parents. He was from a rich upscale family and I was from a middle- to lower-class family. I mean, my family did okay money-wise, but family-wise, we were a mess.

"I married my husband, much to his parents' dismay. We went on to have three more children. He made it possible for me to stay home with my kids, working a lot of overtime. I had to do everything he said. He started hitting my children, especially David. That's when I decided to get out. I did it with the help of my friends on the ambulance service, Sandy and Joe and Marsha. They were the only friends I'd ever been allowed to choose on my own.

"I had one friend then, before I left my husband. Her name was Sue. Our kids were the same age, so we hung out a lot. She was the best cook and her house was immaculate. Mine was not. I felt my children were my job. The house cleaning could wait.

"Before that, I was so isolated, I'd never even written a check. I was married at sixteen and knew nothing. I'd graduated from high school, but didn't know how to cook, grocery-shop, do the banking, or anything else domestic.

"Once I decided to leave, my friends took pictures of my bruises took me to a lawyer, changed the locks, and moved my husband to an apartment all in the same day. My friends taught me these things. And then later, when Marsha and I got together, I was twenty-three. She basically raised me."

"What do you mean, raised you?" Sara asked.

"Well, as I said, I knew nothing when I got married, and learned nothing but how to raise children during that time. My mom was an alcoholic and drug user, so I learned nothing from her except that I didn't want to be like her. She found after a while she could no longer afford the drugs, so she sold me to men in exchange for drugs. I was eleven when this started. She was paid in drugs and alcohol for my body.

"I was sick a lot and went to the doctors frequently. She said we were indigent, so the services were low-cost, or else she wrote bad checks. Then she put me on the pill. I became depressed and cried all the time. She gave me some sort of drugs to make me happy. The doctor said this could have contributed to my bipolar and med resistance."

"I'm sorry I asked," Sara said sadly.

"No problem. You couldn't have known," I said.

*　　　*　　　*

We returned to group, now minus Robert and Patty.

A new person was there, along with a different facilitator for the afternoon session.

"I'd like to introduce myself for those who haven't met me yet," the facilitator said. "I'm Sam. I've been working here ten years. At one time, I was a patient. I was a veteran with PTSD. They helped me a lot. I went to school and became a social worker and came back here. I feel honored they took me. As you can see, we have a new patient. His name is Steve. Would you like to tell us about yourself, Steve?"

Steve seemed a little embarrassed but began to speak. He was choked up as he started.

"My brother and I were best friends. He was twenty-five and I was twenty-three. This happened two years ago. He was my hero. He committed suicide by jumping off an Illinois bridge. It was a tall bridge and the river runs fast, and he couldn't swim. Boaters saw him float soon after. They pulled him out and tried CPR to no avail. I've never gotten over it. My depression got so deep I tried to hang myself. My father found me before I died. My parents didn't put me in counseling. They took away my school tuition and kicked me out.

"I am now homeless. I didn't know what to do. I am still suicidal. I went to the ER. If you want to come to the psych ward, you must go to the ER first, and the wait is about five hours. They take your stuff and if you're suicidal or homicidal they put you in these silly blue paper scrubs that don't fit."

Suddenly the doors opened. All we could see was police officers holding a man in cuffs. We overheard them telling Sam the patient needed a psych eval before going to jail.

We all gasped when it was Robert who walked in.

Sam said, "Robert, you've been gone less than two hours. What happened?"

Robert was agitated and spoke angrily.

"My wife—that bitch—immediately started fighting with me the moment we got home. I tried all those crappy coping skills and they didn't work. She slapped me and punched me and called me a psycho. I couldn't help it. I hit her. She kept fighting so I pushed her; I just wanted to walk away. Her head hit the corner of the cabinet. She didn't wake up, so I called 911. She was still breathing so I just waited for them.

"They came and stabilized her spine and took her away. They said she has a concussion. She still hasn't woken up. They say she has a brain bleed. Since I was here this morning, they brought me back. If I'm okay, they will take me to jail for domestic violence. I'll probably just stay there a few days until she cools off."

Sam said, "Okay, Robert, have a seat. I don't know how long you will be here. The police and your doctor will figure it out.

He then looked toward Jantu. "How are you this afternoon?" Sam asked.

Jantu looked up sadly and started by saying, "I talked to my parents at lunch. Sometimes I hate them. They don't care about me. They care about my brother. He is a cardiac surgeon and a lawyer. He speaks four languages and presents at many conferences. He went to Harvard and I went to University Illinois Chicago medical school. I want to be a surgeon. Whatever I do, it will always come second to my brother. He married an Asian girl and they are expecting their first child. He is living his life exactly how my parents want.

"Now that I am here my parents say I may not get to go back to med school. They are still upset about my upcoming marriage. They want me to marry who they picked for me."

I felt badly for Jantu.

"My partner says your parents look very depressed when they're in the waiting room," I said. "I'm sure they feel badly for you."

"My parents feel badly for themselves," Jantu replied. "What will they tell the neighbors, and their high society

167

friends? Right now, they're telling everyone that I'm helping my sick grandmother. They still want me to stay here until I am 'completely fixed.'

"Throughout my time here I've come to understand that what I've been experiencing are delusions and hallucinations. I may be under too much stress to return to med school now. I'm okay with that for right now."

CHAPTER 47

Routine

Soon we went to supper, followed by free time, then snack, then another group, then showers, then bed. They locked up your clothes. You couldn't have towels or washcloths in your rooms; they gave them to you at the time of your shower. You have to take an evening or morning shower. You have to leave the outer door open while you stand behind a door that covers your middle. I was lucky, as I'm short; I wondered what the tall people did. My legs and head showed, but my private parts and most of my body was covered. When you wanted to dress, you called out to them and they shut the door halfway so you could dress. There was a washer and dryer for when you got your clothes, but most of us were still wearing the paper scrubs, so they were of no use to us.

That night I was allowed to get my clothes back. I loved the comfort of my pajamas, but I noticed they had removed the drawstring, just as they had removed my shoelaces. I was okay with that, because at least I had my belongings back. Some writing paper, a half of a pencil (no pens or full-sized pencils?), my Bible, and my clothes. Oh, how I had missed my own comfy socks and slippers. Some people had not packed a bag, or else they had no one to bring them their things, so they were forced to remain in the blue paper scrubs.

When we got our snack, it was quite the big deal. You wanted to be first in line because sometimes you could get an ice-cream sandwich. If you were last it was a piece of fruit. So of course I always shoved my way to the front of the line.

When it was time for bed, we all went like lemmings to our rooms. I lay in the dark wishing I were home. Marsha would understand all of this and would be able to help me, but my counselor told me I shouldn't put that burden on her.

Soon I fell asleep. The drugs they gave me made me fall asleep easily.

That was part of my issue. If I didn't sleep, I could be awake for five days straight. After that I would start to see things. You can only go for a short while without sleep. That's why they use that as a punishment for prisoners. I would go into a manic episode where I would spend excessively. Other people gambled, drank, had sex, things like that. When I say I spent excessively, I mean, two cars; a bedroom set; furniture for the kitchen. I couldn't pay for; it all went on my credit card. And this was only part of my mania.

I tended toward the more-depressed side of bipolar. I was depressed most of the time. I couldn't get out of my miserable mood, and finally the doctor suggested electroconvulsive therapy, known as shock therapy. I thought of One Flew Over the Cuckoo's Nest. I was apprehensive, to say the least.

*   *   *

One day at group, Sam said sternly, "I need to talk about an incident that happened at lunch. It was noted that two people left the lunch area and went to a patient's room. You are not allowed in other people's rooms. All kinds of things could happen, and many of you are hurt and vulnerable. Being here takes away your right to make those decisions. We expect this will not continue, but from now on, to be safe, the women will be seated together, as will the men."

We all changed seats to sit in our designated areas.

When we were settled, Steve asked, "How can I make sure my parents can't find me here?"

Some of us were worried about the same thing.

Sam said, "Remember the code word you gave when you got here? No one can talk to you or even know you are here unless they have your code word."

Steven said, "I don't think my life will ever be back together. When I was younger, my brother and I were inseparable. Where one of us was, there was the other as well. Our parents left us alone a lot. He taught me how to ride a bike, catch frogs, play golf and baseball, how to kiss a girl.

"When he was twelve, he started hanging around with a bunch of older kids. They started teasing me but my brother made them stop. Everyone listened to and respected him. I willingly went to all his ball games just to cheer him on.

"My brother drove me everywhere, whether we were where we were 'supposed' to be or not. He caught me smoking once and slapped me so hard. He said, 'I hope that smokes your face! The next time I catch you or hear of you smoking I'll make you eat the whole pack!' Boy, was he mad. He never hit me intentionally after that.

"My brother was the favorite. He was the golden boy. He was the one who told me our mom was mentally ill. She always hated me. I remember her trying to drown me in the tub when I was four. My brother saved me. That was the first of many times my mother 'went away for a while.' My brother told me she just needed some 'quiet time.'

Sam said, "That must have been very difficult for you. That explains why your parents threw you out after your brother was gone. Hopefully we can help you here."

*　　　*　　　*

At another session one day, Kate said, "Sara, you look like you want to say something."

"Yes. I was just thinking how parents can screw up their kids. I remember being five years old and standing in front of the mirror and twirling around. I liked doing that because my dress looked like a cake. It was made up of a bunch of pastel colors, and my grandma called it a 'sherbet dress.' The sleeves flew like butterflies. My dad called me over and picked me up, holding my butt in his hand.

171

'How's my pretty-pretty princess?' he said. 'You look beautiful. If you were twenty years older, I'd marry you myself. Give your daddy some love.' He pulled me tight to him. I was so happy. My dad took me into the kitchen to watch my mom and the maid getting everything set up for a party. Then he carried me back to the foyer. It was so perfect.

"I didn't think anything of it when he asked me to pull down my panties. He didn't touch me, but he looked at me long enough to make me feel uncomfortable.

"I went to a special kind of school. In second grade I was on a waiting list and my parents were very glad when I was chosen to attend. We didn't have to sit in desks all the time. We had stations. Like sand, water, balloons, puzzles, numbers, colors, alphabet, and a bunch of other stuff. My dad was always late picking me up. I didn't find out until later that he was seeing his mistress during that time.

"I was kidnapped when I was ten. A neighbor girl, Sheri, and I were friends. One day her brother, who was sixteen, asked me to go to the movies with him and his sister. I went to the car and got in, waiting for my friend. I remember the seat was fuzzy and blue. Sheri's brother Mike got in the car. He started the car and took off. He told me Sheri was running late and his mom was bringing her later.

"He drove out of town to a dark and run-down shed. It smelled like fish, and I could hear running water nearby, like a river or a lake. He made me lie on the floor and he just lay on top of me. We both had our clothes on. I was afraid I would get splinters from the floor.

"We stayed there for twelve hours. It was never handled by the police. They didn't want Sheri's brother to go jail! My mom and dad chose to deal with me by ignoring me. They blamed me for getting in the car alone with him. It was as if I made them aware of their own guilt."

*   *   *

Kate asked, "How are you feeling today, Jantu?"

We all looked over at her.

"My psychosis is over and I'm back to reality," Jantu said. "I hope my parents will be happy about this. They've always been proud people. My dad is a self-made millionaire. He's in the technical investments field. He has done well for himself. My mother has been a stay-at-home mom. She pushed my brother and me to excel in everything. We had the 'perfect family.' They lived within their means and owed no one. They have several extra rooms in our house for various aunts, uncles, grandparents, and so forth. Eventually my grandparents will live with us. That is part of our culture. Sometimes we'd have a full house.

"My mom was always in the thick of things. I was always on the outs. They loved my brother and treated him like a 'golden boy' whereas I was just 'spare parts.' My brother had cancer when he was younger and I was created in case I was a match for my brother. Turns out I was a perfect match. I don't remember all the hassle of the whole thing, but my 'spare parts' saved him."

"That sounds terrible—like a lot to live up to," Kelly said. "Is that why you have so much stress in your life?"

Jantu just nodded as tears slid from the corners of her eyes.

*   *   *

It was Kelly's turn.

"I am an anxious person, as I've said. I am fearful of everything. It wasn't always this way. I remember going to the theater, museums, book readings, and art shows. My husband travels for a living. He is my second husband. The first one died. He sells electronic adaptations for the disabled. He's a good man. We've been married fifteen years. He's never even thought of cheating. We used to have fun together.

"One night when he was gone the dog was going crazy. Barking his head off. I finally had to lock him in his cage. I checked all the doors and found them all locked. We live in a town of twenty-five hundred people. No one locks their doors, garages, cars, or anything. I lock mine because I'm alone. Sometimes I leave a window open to get a cross breeze to cool the house off with the night air. Saves on air-conditioning.

"That night I thought I'd closed the window, but evidently, I had not. I got a glass of water and started upstairs. I went up to my bathroom, peed, and washed my face. I went back to the bedroom and removed my robe and started to get into bed. It was the floor creaking that gave me the first clue that something was amiss.

"I felt the gloved hand over my mouth and a low voice saying, 'Don't scream. I want jewelry, drugs, and money. Scream and you're dead; keep calm and you live.' He had a ski mask, hoodie, and a gun. He said, 'I'm removing my hand—now remember no screaming. Dump out your jewelry box on your left side of your bed.'

"I started to cry and asked if I could keep my daughter's ring, because it was all I had left of her. She was fifteen when she died. He examined the ring, which was worthless, but had sentimental value.

"'I suppose it's okay,' he said. 'It's worth nothing to me.' Next he wanted to see the closet. He told me that he'd overheard me the other day, telling someone that I hide money from my husband in the closet. 'You need to be careful what you say in public,' he said to me, and added, 'Now be a nice lady and go get it for me." It was twenty-eight hundred dollars. 'Is that all you have?' he asked. 'I don't want to find out you're lying.' I told him it was all I had. Next, we went to the gun safe. All in all, he took two guns, the cash, and the gold jewelry.

"But the most important thing he took was my security. He raped me before he left that night."

We all sat there in silence, horrified.

"I never told anyone except my husband. He blamed me for talking about our finances in public, for cashing the checks and not depositing them in the bank right away, for not taking the gun with me downstairs, for leaving the window open, and for not reporting the rape. Still, he loves me and has tried to get over it. I have become overly cautious, anxious, and pretty much agoraphobic since then.

"Later I found I was pregnant. We didn't know if the baby was my husband's or the rapist's. I carried the baby to full term. When the baby was born, my husband took a DNA test and found out the baby wasn't his, so he insisted we give the baby up for adoption. I felt torn, but knew ultimately it was the best for the baby. I would always be watching to see if he was anything like his father, the rapist. Either way, I was sad. My husband understood and brought me here for treatment.

"But on the drive over here, he asked, 'Why would you want a monster baby?'"

CHAPTER 48

Final Days

A couple days later, there was another knock on the door. It was the same police officers. They told Robert his wife had died and now he was facing murder charges.

He argued that he wasn't in his right mind at the time the event occurred. He said she had started the fight and she drove him to push her. He was taken to see the psychiatrist. The police stayed outside the door and waited to speak to the psychiatrist, after which they left and Robert stayed. None of us knew what was going to happen to Robert.

Jantu's parents took her home that night, as she was no longer having psychotic/schizophrenic symptoms. They said she wouldn't be returning to the psych ward for any additional counseling; it was an internal matter, and the family could fix her. She would be having a wedding in two weeks, marrying the man they had picked for her.

Sara ending up gaining weight, but not enough to be released. She continued to walk the halls with her IV pole, refusing to eat very much.

Patty did indeed return the next day. She came in and said, "I told you I'd be back!" The social worker found a nursing home that would accept Patty. Later I heard she was happy and had made some friends.

Steve received treatment and was released with medication. Problem was, he was homeless. They dropped him off at the Morningstar shelter. I told him he could come to our house. He was released on Friday and I didn't go home until the following Monday. When I went to the shelter I was told I couldn't go in, because it was a men's shelter. I asked if Steven was there and they said "No." Later on, I came to my senses, realizing that you don't take someone into your home from the psych ward. That's like meeting someone in jail or at an AA meeting and having them come and stay with you.

Kelly went home to her husband and continued both individual and couples counseling.

*   *   *

I left after two weeks and three days. Considering it was a short-term place, my stay of seventeen days was a long time. They decided I needed to have electroconvulsive shock therapy. When they do ECT, they take you to the procedure room and you're lying on a gurney. I could hear the sounds of other people getting the treatment. I heard patients talking and then I heard the electric buzzing that sounded like a fast Star Wars droid.

When it was my turn they came and strapped me down. They put these electrodes on my head. The ECT induces a seizure. They put a bite guard between my teeth because without it, I could bite my tongue or crack a tooth. They did a total of twelve sessions. It finally took care of the depression, but also wiped part of my memory that I've never gotten back. The medications I was given for bipolar initially made me sleepy and lose my creativity.

The social worker asked Marsha to go do some Christmas shopping while they finished getting me ready to be discharged. Marsha was worried about how we would afford the medication. The social worker was no help.

I rode home on the floorboard of the car. I was embarrassed, scared, and agoraphobic.

*   *   *

That year there were no presents, no decorations, and no tree. We celebrated Christmas, just Marsha and me, sitting in the dark staring at the TV. The kids had their own homes and lives. We just stared, not realizing what was on.

It had been a tough year. Marsha had been dealing with several health issues of her own.

She has had nine back surgeries, and it has taken away a lot of her ability to walk. She has also had four shoulder operations, one surgery on her Achilles tendon, and one ganglion cyst.

Once when she came home from adult church camp, she was acting senile. After consulting with three of my friends, Lin, MaryAnn, and Barb, we determined that we needed to take her to the hospital. She waited in the ER for seven hours. They took a CT but not a blood sugar test. Then they did labs and noted that her blood sugar was high. Your blood sugar is supposed to be 70 to 110; hers was 1,200.

They sent her off to critical care. She had started hallucinating. She thought she was in a chocolate fire truck on the Oprah show, long since canceled. (I guess Oprah had actually featured this truck on her show years ago.)

Marsha went to a nursing home for several days after her hospitalization. She was still hallucinating. When she was there, she put her call light on in the middle of the night and this giant man came in to take her to the bathroom. She was cured on the spot! She called me the next morning and said, "Get me the hell out of here. No giant man is going to wipe my ass." (She is a very shy person.)

Because she had such difficulties walking, the kids and I were ever conscious of potential obstacles for her. One night we were at the country club, our favorite eating establishment. When we got up to leave we noticed a French fry on the floor. The first person who passed it thought, "Oh no, I hope Marsha sees that French fry." The second person thought, "Oh, I wonder if I should stop and pick that up?" Then I came along and thought, "Here, let me kick that French fry out of the way so Marsha doesn't trip."

Marsha, walking next to me, leaned to the right to avoid the French fry and promptly set her cane down on it, which made her lean forward. I caught her and spun her around, trying to "save her." We promptly crashed into a drunk person who said, "Hey, hey! Watch out!"

We apologized, then laughed, because here we were, two old ladies about to get beaten up by a drunk over a French fry.

We went to the car where our children waited, wondering what the heck was going on.

*   *   *

I saw other families who had Christmas pictures taken so I decided we would, too. I made everyone wear white shirts with black vests and pants. Despite the photographer's reservations, that's the picture we had taken. A month later we received the very large portrait. I should have listened to the photographer: We looked like the Partridge Family.

Every year the kids had school pictures taken. One year Brandy decided to pull her curly hair back, leaving just one piece loose. Right down the middle of her face. I'm going to put that picture on the front page of the paper when she turns forty. She is thirty-nine now, and not long ago broke up with her boyfriend of ten years. He just stopped going places and paying attention to her. She found someone else who gave her what she needed, and now they are engaged. I guess that means you should never neglect your partner, because it makes them wither and wilt. Use good manners, say please and thank you, and always take time to listen. I've always told my children to say, "I love you—wear your seat belt," even if you're mad, because you never know when they might be gone.

I think that's why Marsha and I still get along. We have always had respect for each other, and after all these years we are still in love. We never hit below the belt even in the worst of fights. And actually, we no longer really fight or argue. Sometimes we will give a long sigh, which means it's time to ask the other person "Are you okay? What's wrong?"

Marsha is not a jealous person. She lets me do what I want, within reason. She doesn't like me to drink a lot, and driving drunk is a definite no-no. We saw too many people who were the victims of drunk driving. I guess in the beginning I tried to find ways to make her jealous. I flirted with other women and men. She always said that if I wanted someone else, to go ahead and go for it. I was hurt. I thought it meant she didn't care enough to fight for me. Eventually I learned that she knew I'd never leave because ultimately, I adore her. We share the same values about parenting, religion, work ethic, honesty, and much more. We love each other so much it's crazy. People envy our relationship.

CHAPTER 49

It's Hell Getting Old

Seems like we spend every day at a doctor's appointment for one thing or another.

Marsha is having very strange medical symptoms. She has started saying her forehead is stiff. Then she started having this stiffness in her chin and lips. She falls asleep mid-sentence and does this many times a day. She has been to many specialists, with no good answers. It's not MS, Parkinson's, ALS, or Alzheimer's, which is all good. I think she is narcoleptic and has a ruptured disk in her neck.

In May 2019, I noticed a pain in my right breast. It was time for my annual mammogram so I set up an appointment. They called me later telling me to prepare for an ultrasound just in case. I arrived on the appointed day and place, the women's suite at St. James Hospital in Pontiac, Illinois. It's a beautiful place, with bottled water and snacks, its own bathroom, and its own ultrasound. The technician had a patient ahead of me, so I watched HGTV while I waited. Soon it was my turn. I entered the mammography room. The lady was very nice.

"Scoot up to the machine," she told me. She apologized for her cold hands. (They weren't.) She took my left boob and laid it on the flat cold plate while placing my arms above me across the machine. She moved a flat plate on top of the boob. I started laughing, as I thought Oh, a boob sandwich. I quickly stopped laughing and started wincing, as the plates were moving tighter and tighter. My boob became as flat as a tortilla. I have a high pain tolerance, as I think nothing is worse than one of my bad migraines. I watched, fascinated that my big boobs could be that flat.

I felt sorry for smaller-breasted women. I bet they have a worse time. That's the curse they get for being skinny.

I said, "My boobs breastfed four babies and I'm in a long-term relationship, so I'm not afraid." I was sent out to wait in the waiting room while the radiologist looked at the films. I thought that was weird, because they usually let me go, saying they will call me if they need a re-scan; otherwise, a letter will arrive.

So, I waited. I was called for a re-scan. She took all kinds of shots of the left breast and a few of the right.

Again, I waited. She called me back in from the waiting room and said, "The radiologist wants an ultrasound." We did the ultrasound and the radiologist wanted a biopsy. So that was scheduled.

On the day of the biopsy I was nervous. I was afraid they would put a needle through my nipple. I know people get these areas pierced all the time, but it was never my cup of tea. My radiologist was very good and told me everything she was going to do. She said she would take pieces from all around the area of concern.

Five days later, I was called by my ob-gyn. Not my primary and not the oncologist. I only see my ob-gyn every five years, as I've had a partial hysterectomy. I suspected something was amiss. I still don't remember all he said, but he was very nice about it. He said "malignancy" as supportively as he could. He discussed the tumors and options. He said, "There is another area in the same breast that we'll watch, and check every six months."

"Hell no, we are not 'watching' anything," I said.

The radiologist, although extremely nice, had thought the area was "probably benign." I was taking no chances. I wanted it all gone.

I was fatigued and nauseous. I hadn't even had the surgery yet. That was six days away. I was planning for the removal of both breasts and wearing prosthetics.

Wednesday arrived and the surgeon, Dr. Windsome, met with me before the surgery and again discussed my options: a lumpectomy, mastectomy, or bilateral mastectomy. I told her I wanted to do the bilateral. I told her I was too anxious, and with my bipolar I would always worry, every day, if something else would be found.

We continued with my choice. My insurance was on board, so I was set.

I went into nuclear medicine at eight a.m. after having to be there an hour beforehand, plus an hour-long drive to get there. I had been up since four-thirty a.m. Marsha was taken to a waiting room where she could "relax" until I got done.

After nine hours, she was finally advised she could go to the room. Marsha told me, "They can't take the breathing tube out because your oxygen would drop." Later that day the tube was removed and I was placed on oxygen.

After we were situated in the room, the nurse came in and explained the various tubes I had coming from my body. She told me I was a fall risk and couldn't get up by myself. I slept for that day and part of the next. Luckily Marsha could watch the news on TV and play games on her electronic technology thingy. She has been playing "Township" for three years. I couldn't do anything for three years except eat chocolate.

I ran a temp the next day that required an additional day there. We were ready to be home, because my machines were beeping all the time. The last night they finally moved my IV so I had less beeping to deal with. All the nurses and technicians were great, but I was ready to "take leave" of the place.

The next day we got to go home. So, with all the accessories I had been given along the way, we were pushed to the exit door.

Marsha does not walk well even with her two canes. I have told her I am getting older and can't always do everything she needs. She has finally humbled herself to admit that she is unable to do all the things she used to. She was always so strong and independent; she took it hard when she had to ask for help.

When I got home from surgery after the double mastectomy, I peeked under the elastic bandage and saw my deflated boobs with a horizontal scar across both and drains at the sides. I was in pain. I popped some meds and went to bed. Marsha was glad to have her electric soft recliner back. I slept the rest of the day away into the next morning.

I went to see Dr. Windsome two weeks later. I am amazed whenever I see her. With her thin frame and long hair, she is pretty and intelligent and has a good bedside manner. She was so nice to call me at home with the good news that I wouldn't need chemo or radiation.

I had a bad sprain in my upper back. I used a heating pad on it. The back pain was worse than the mastectomy pain. The "breasts" were more numb than painful. The back pain lasted a month.

Two days later I had to have a bath. This was allowed if I sat backwards while someone gave me a shower and shampoo. There was more water on the floor than on me, but it was better than nothing. My hair was finally clean. I couldn't use deodorant so close to the drains. Each "breast" had a drain coming out of it. The drains exited out of the "side boobs." I had bigger "side boobs" than the average small-breasted woman.

"Will these side boobs go away?" I inquired.

"Not necessarily," Dr. Windsome answered. "Remember I told you about this possibility?" She had told me about a lot of possibilities. I'd forgotten that issue, but it was okay. I had been firm in my decision. I still was. Some women go through depression and remorse and a host of other feelings. I didn't. I think it's a personal decision and only the woman experiencing this disease can choose the best outcome for themselves.

I don't have any regrets except now food goes down the front of my shirt and lands on my belly instead of my boobs. I continue to pick chicken breading out of my belly button. I've noticed I have no appetite. I am nauseous all the time. The only kind of food I will eat is Tyson honey chicken strips. I eat them for breakfast, lunch, and dinner.

CHAPTER 50

Friendships

I have terrific friends, Lucy, Tabitha, and Ray. We are a close-knit bunch, hard workers and self-motivated. We laugh, joke, and talk about what's happened in our lives since we last saw each other. We share our problems and successes, from the ordinary to much deeper conversations.

We also smoke marijuana together. They offered me the chance to smoke many times and I always said no. But eventually I gave in when I was in a lot of physical pain. I talked to my pastor about it and he says the Bible doesn't mention it. It took away my pain like no other pain medication ever had, including opioids. I'd never smoked so I didn't know how to inhale. I usually coughed and coughed and coughed. It made my mouth very dry.

Ray is in his twenties and goes to Illinois State University, mostly to party with his friends. He is taking general electives until he decides what he wants to do. He laughs a lot, showing his straight white teeth. He makes me laugh, and I really like him. He's charming and motivated—a cool person who is kind and helps everyone. When we smoke together Ray shows off some cool tricks he can do with smoke, like blowing smoke rings. He lays his head on the table and exhales the smoke onto the table, so it looks like fog. Then he puts his hand through it and it makes a tornado. I learn something new from him every day.

Tabitha is like Switzerland. She sees all sides of a story and never plays favorites. She doesn't argue with anyone. She knows her own mind. She is cautious, kind, and reliable.

Lucy owns a boutique. She makes jams and handmade quiltes, and has all kinds of jewelry. She is such a kind and loving person, and accepts everyone. She is pretty, wise, and gives good advice.

We have Sunday dinner together every week. Sometimes Ray's friend, Eli, will join us. We often talk about deep questions and issues when we're together, a way to understand each other better. I'm usually the one asking the questions because I am older than they are, and tend to question everything.

One day I asked, "What is your position in this group?"

Everyone agreed Lucy is the boss. Tabitha is the laid-back one, and Ray provides the younger point of view and is the eye candy. Me? I'm the mom and the one who ponders and talks about my medical issues too much.

Next question: "Favorite gift as a kid?"

Lucy, who is in her fifties, remembers she loved her children's sewing machine. Tabitha's favorite was a Cabbage Patch doll. She is in her early forties. For Ray, in his twenties, it was expensive sneakers or a family trip to Disney. My answer was easy: my Malibu Barbie Camper. Which my sister promptly stood on and broke.

Next question: "How many sexual partners have you had?"

Lucy said, "At least thirteen." (I was amazed.) Tabitha said, "Eleven." Ray answered, "Four." Me: "Two men and one woman."

The reason I asked these questions was to see the world through their eyes, feeling that they are more up-to-date on current norms and morals.

These questions led to more questions.

I asked, "Have you ever found a soulmate?"

The girls answered "no," but Tabitha said she was content anyway, while Ray and I both answered "yes."

Unfortunately, Ray had recently broken up with his girlfriend of three years. He found out that she had been cheating on him with multiple people while they were going together. At first, he'd thought they would get married; alas, no. He thought the breakup was his fault until he found out she had cheated. His sorrow turned to anger, but also relief. (They would reconcile months later.)

I expanded on my answer by saying Marsha was my soulmate. We've been through everything together. Sickness, health, rich and poor (mostly poor). Even getting lost when someone read the map wrong.

I asked them what they view as their best attributes.

Lucy thought for a minute and said, "I'm kindhearted, I work hard, I'm friendly and well-liked. I wear my heart on my sleeve, though I try to disguise it in my strength as a woman." We all agreed.

Tabitha went next. "I'm laid-back, understanding, and open-minded. But I love hard and hate hard. I hold grudges. In some cases, I can't forgive and forget." I wouldn't have guessed that last part, as I've never even seen her mad.

Ray: "I'm a gentleman, respectable, fun." (He is all this and more.)

Me: "I think too much and too deeply. I'm too sensitive, a caretaker, and a list maker."

We each have our role in the group, and that is what makes it interesting and keeps our relationships to each other strong. I've created the family I want to replace the family I grew up with.

* * *

Marsha and I also have lots of friends at church: Cheryl, who has eight kids and homeschools them. Before I met her and her kids, I thought all homeschooled kids were weird. Hers are nice and very down-to-earth, just like Cheryl.

Then there's Barb, the go-to person for everything at church. I just happened to have worked with her at my state job. I loved her then and do now.

Tina, Loretta, and Larry, whom I've mentioned before, drive us places when we are sick or have surgeries. Loretta and Larry are like Energizer Bunnies, even though they are in their late seventies.

Cheri is a relatively new friend. She's very sweet and understands chronic diseases. She and her husband, Paul, were so kind and helpful when Marsha had her last surgery.

Marielle—or Mars, as she is called—always checks up on us and brings us food from Arby's, where she works. I go to fabric stores with Lin, and she drives us to the airport when we travel. I'm in a weekly Bible study group with Janee, Becky, and Evelyn. My friend Chris helps us with groceries and housekeeping, things like mopping the floor.

Most people are not as lucky as we are. We are truly blessed. All of these friends are dear to my heart.

CHAPTER 51

My Kids

My kids are all grown now. David went to the US Naval Academy and became a systems engineer. This includes nuclear, electrical, and mechanical engineering. He's also strong as an ox. He separated from the navy after he completed his obligation. He found out about a targeted individual issue within the government. You can look him up on Facebook if you are interested. There is so much information on the topic and he wants to write his own book. So, I'll leave it at that. He works at the University of Chicago while living next door to us. He also works at a business where he moves furniture and other items from location to location. He is also studying to be a day trader. At this point he is too busy for a relationship and kids.

Brandy has three beautiful daughters, Kenley, Coraline, and Suri, and is a supervisor at Walmart. She lives with a Walmart manager, James. She and her ex, Rickey, co-parent well. They both understand the need to be the best parents for the girls. So far, so good. She got engaged last Christmas. Like her mother, she also writes and reads a lot.

Daniel was also in the navy. He had a traditional church wedding the first time. She was beautiful and they looked like they had just walked out of a magazine. Ultimately she was unfaithful and they divorced. I still like her. After all, she is the mother of my grandchild. We found out about his second marriage via social media when he was deployed to Hawaii. Daniel has one child from his first wife and two from his second wife. His second wife had three when they got together, so altogether he has six kids. His wife, Sara, homeschools the older kids. (God love her!) He is gone most nights but is home almost every day sleeping. He is—you guessed it—a truck driver. He's a great dad.

Daniel Jr. was the first grandbaby on both sides of the family. He was spoiled like crazy. When he was born, I opened my heart, and my checkbook. Once when he was a toddler, he was traveling with us. He'd recently had the chicken pox vaccine and started throwing up in the van. Marsha just yelled, "We got barf!"

"What? Barf! Oh my gosh!"

I pulled over as quickly as possible. I cleaned the car with paper towels while Marsha stripped Baby Daniel down to a diaper and bathed him in water from the cooler. People honked as they went by. That helped Daniel, because we told him everyone was proud of him.

As the first grandchild, he knew he was adorable. We gave him a hand mirror to occupy himself once during a long drive. It kept him enthralled for hours, just making faces and smiling at his teeth. He is still a little vain.

All in all the kids and the grandkids are doing great. Coming from their mom and grandma, you know it must be true.

CHAPTER 52

More Medical Issues

Four weeks after surgery, I thought I had an infection of the left breast. I went to my primary doctor and showed him the area and he put me on an antibiotic. Six weeks after surgery the wound started to drain and looked "icky." I started running a fever of nearly 103 degrees. Marsha drove the sixty miles to Bloomington, Illinois, where Dr. Windsome looked at the wound and determined she needed to clean it out with a surgical procedure, which she did on an outpatient basis. It felt much better after the procedure. My surgeon is the greatest.

When I found out about the surgery, I called my grandson who told his mother I was getting my vasectomy redone. This prompted a call from Daniel to Marsha asking what was going on.

A couple of days later I received a wound vac. This is a vacuum that sucks the blood and dead tissue into a canister. It is much better than a wet to dry dressing because the dressing pulls the good skin off. It also keeps the wound from bleeding though the dressing. It is changed by the home health nurse three times per week. Both my boobs hurt now, even though there's not much there anymore.

*   *   *

Marsha and I are both brittle diabetics. Our sugars go up and down, up and down. Marsha sees many doctors, each with their own specialty and ability to "tweak" her meds.

Once, after fifteen days of hard coughing we finally took Marsha to the ER. Her legs and feet were swollen, along with her hands and stomach. (My stomach is always swollen. Yeah, I'm going with that.) She was hospitalized with bacterial and aspiration pneumonia. She was already on an antibiotic and was given two more in the ER. She also had an echocardiogram which showed congestive heart failure. They gave her Lasix and she dropped twenty-four pounds in three days. What a diet! Too bad she had to do it the hard way. She had two sleep studies with no definitive answers except to try a CPAP machine. I think most of America has sleep apnea (when you stop breathing) or desaturates (oxygen decreases) in their sleep.

Recently, Marsha got shingles on the right side of her face and eye. She fell at home soon after that, so we went off to the ER in Pontiac, twenty miles away. We didn't know it, but we were about to learn the cause of Marsha's condition, after almost a year.

When we got to the ER, we discussed our fears relating to Marsha's ongoing medical issues with the ER doctor, saying we thought it was herniation in her neck that was causing all the trouble. The doctor listened to us and did a CT scan. After looking at the results, the doctor advised Marsha she was not going home but was being transferred to a larger OSF hospital in Bloomington. She would go by ambulance, and I would meet her there.

I kissed her good-bye and we said I love you to each other. I went and grabbed some McDonald's for the forty-mile trip to Bloomington. I don't drive well in the dark, and this, coupled with the fact that it was a foggy night, made for a dangerous drive. My face pressed to the windshield and my chest practically on the steering wheel, I drove twenty-five miles an hour the whole way to Bloomington. Even so, I arrived before the ambulance.

Entering the ER at St. Joseph Medical Center I noticed the smell right away—you know the one, of alcohol wipes and sanitized something or other. I asked the security guard if Marsha was going to the ER or a room. They gave me a room number on the neurology floor, so I went up there and waited. I told the nurses at the desk that Marsha would be arriving and that she had shingles on her face. They immediately told me to wait in a waiting room. The nurse walked down the hall to Marsha's room and started assembling gowns, gloves, and masks. The "Isolation" sign on the door looked ominous.

I was relieved I'd already had shingles, although I learned later that it is possible to get them again. I figured since I'd been around her for weeks already, I probably wasn't going to get them.

The next day an MRI was done. The surgeon came up and said, "We are going to have to do surgery tomorrow. You have two massive disk herniations in your neck at the C3-4 and C5-6, and we need to take care of this."

Of course we agreed, and surgery was set for the next day.

*　　*　　*

On the day of her procedure I waited from 11:00 a.m. until 7:00 p.m. in the surgical waiting room. The surgeon finally came out and advised me that although she'd had a spinal fluid leak during the surgery, Marsha was doing fine now, and should continue to improve.

I stayed with her the whole time she was in the hospital, sleeping in a recliner near her bed that killed my back. I always woke up in pain. I did that at home, too, but it was worse in the hospital.

Marsha went home three days after surgery. Going home depended on whether she could pee and poop. She has a very shy bladder and wasn't able to pee for two days. My bladder would have burst.

Marsha would have been released even more quickly if she hadn't experienced hallucinations again. This time she was eating cookies that were not there. I watched her for a while and then asked, "What are you eating?"

She smiled and replied, "An Oreo—but it's not double-stuff." She would shake the crumbs from her hand and then wipe the rest of the imaginary cookie on her pants.

"Is it an air cookie?" I inquired.

"Nope," she said, "I got it off the filthy floor."

So, I did what any good spouse would do: I started videotaping her. I showed it to her later when she got well and she thought it was hilarious.

A weird thing happened after her surgery. Her leg that had been very swollen for nearly a year returned to a normal size. It was quite surprising, since everyone said she had everything from cellulitis to congestive heart failure. Turns out, she had neither.

We were so happy when she returned home and started physical therapy. Before the surgery she couldn't lift her foot above a sheet of paper, and after PT she could lift her foot high enough to tie her own shoes. She did better after this surgery than she did after any of the other seven she's had. She still walks poorly with two canes, but somehow remains the world's greatest optimist. In the few hours of the night when she dreams, she can walk normally; it's only when she awakens that the reality of pain hits her.

Being a caretaker isn't easy. Helping with showers, tying her shoes, doing the laundry, cleaning the house and cooking. As I mentioned before, I can't cook. I bought a lot of canned ravioli, soup, and ramen noodles. She had very little appetite, which was good for me. I lived on popcorn for a month because I didn't like the abovementioned foods.

We are content even though we live with more sickness than health. We are still in love, and say "I love you" several times per day, and mean it. We live like two old spinster sisters.

Our house isn't immaculate anymore. Right now, we live out of laundry baskets, but we don't care as much anymore, since we've both had our share of medical issues. Our finances may be short at the end of each month—the medical co-pays and the cost of insulin are brutal—but our oldest son, David, helps us out and we pay him back when the next check comes.

CHAPTER 53

Things That Make Me Go "Hmmm"

1. How do you be both a mother and a friend to your older kids?
2. When we get lost while driving in our car, we turn the radio down.
3. When you overdraw by $2.70, they charge you $25.00. If you don't have the $2.70, how will you pay the bank fee?
4. You must have your glasses to find your glasses if you lose them.
5. If you wear glasses, you hear better with them on. Just goes to show you how much we read lips.
6. You can't jog in my town; if you do, everyone asks you if you need a ride. Why would anybody run for no reason? Except if there is a sale on chocolate.
7. You also can't jog in the street because a farm implement might run you over.
8. Why do you have to pee one last time before leaving the house? This may not happen to the younger generation; maybe just older people like me.
9. Why do people say "old-timers' disease" or "all-timers"? It's Alzheimer's.
10. Why, when you're ready to go from a restaurant, do you stand up and grab another drink of soda?
11. Where do all the unmatched socks go?
12. Why doesn't it snow on Christmas but it does snow on Palm Sunday?

13. Why do I need to ask "Why?" about everything?
14. Why does it always rain on Halloween?
15. Why does the dog throw up just before company comes?
16. Why does every person's watch have a different time?
17. Why are all the store sizes different? I go to one store and I'm a 22, then I go to another store and it's a size 1.
18. Why do I go into a room and forget what I went in there for? It's usually the kitchen, so I just eat some thing while I'm there.
19. Why, when I have to pee, does seeing the toilet makes it worse?
20. Why can't Chinese restaurants make good chocolate desserts?
21. Why, when I was younger, did no one have peanut allergies?
22. Why did my parents have this giant glass ashtray on their coffee table along with a big coffee-table book that no one read?
23. Why did my mother-in-law wash tinfoil when she was a millionaire?
24. Why do people smell and not brush their teeth?
25. Why do people look over their glasses instead of through them?
26. Why do people keep their houses a mess? Especially millennium kids. Were they not Y2K-compatible?
27. Why do people assume a nurse wanted to be a doctor but couldn't make it through med school?
28. Why does a certain cruise line use a song that's about drugs? I can't remember which one, but I get the song stuck in my head.
29. What hair color do bald people put on their drivers' licenses?
30. Do prison buses have an emergency exit?
31. How can you look up a word in a dictionary if you don't know how to spell it?

32. Why do they have letters in math but no numbers in the alphabet? I hated algebra.
33. Why do people who love algebra hate geometry and vice versa?
34. Why are all my friends hilarious and even-tempered? (I know; I'm blessed.)
35. If tomatoes are a fruit, is ketchup a smoothie? (Bad joke.)
36. How come some of my friends chain-smoke and I can't smell it, yet others smell like smoke all the time even if they only smoke only occasionally?
37. How come a person who has a toothache puts an aspirin on their tooth? You don't put an aspirin on your head if you have a headache.
38. Why did Ron have to die of a heart attack at age fifty-seven?

CHAPTER 54

Death

Yes, Ron died way too young.

He was out fixing a trampoline for five of his kids. These kids were from a second wife, Bailey. It was a hot day. He went inside to get a drink and then lay on the couch. He got back up and told his brother-in-law, "I'm tired, but I think I have another twenty years left in me."

He died five hours later. He had a seizure, came around for a short time, and then had a fatal heart attack. His oldest son Jeremy started CPR. The ambulance was called and the EMTs continued CPR, to no avail.

His young wife called me and I was in shock. All I could say was "Really? Really?"

I guess my sister Roxy and cousin Jo were devastated and let out howls at learning the news. Folks thought I didn't care because my reaction was not what they thought it should be. In fact, I was probably more devastated than anyone else because of the relationship Ron and I shared as children.

He was cremated. I realize I did not get closure because of this.

I grieved for two years until suddenly I woke up and realized Enough is enough. I can't stop living because he died.

My cousin Thad had died a few days earlier than Ron from a recurring brain tumor we'd thought had been cured five years prior. He went blind, along with a multitude of other symptoms. It was not a surprise when he passed, but we were all grieving just the same. I would go on to lose my niece (Roxy's daughter) to drugs and my nephew (Ronnie's son) to cancer within the same twelve months. What a rough year.

Marsha sat next to me while I cried and grieved the loss of my family members. My family of origin doesn't speak to me today. I think it's because I told Roxy after the death of her daughter that it wasn't her fault. Or later, when I told her I didn't need family drama anymore. Maybe she took that to mean I didn't care about her and the loss of her daughter, which was not true.

My brother's wife doesn't speak to me either. I called her house one time after Ron died. I was off the wall. I don't remember the actual call because I was going through a major depression. She has since blocked all my calls. I understand her need to protect her children, but I miss them, and her.

Our cousin JoJo was raised as Roxy's twin, so JoJo feels the same way about me that Roxy does.

My sister Rachael was ostracized by the whole family years ago. We tried many times to help her through her drug addiction and when she lost custody of her children. She often told us that everything would be okay if we just left her alone. So finally, we did.

Sometimes I think I am the cause of all of this, but I'm not sure what I can do about it.

CHAPTER 55

Pondering

I've always wondered how my mother felt about this life I've led—her grandchildren, my partner, my true survival. She never seemed to care very much, but I'm happy, whereas I don't think she ever was.

There have been many times I've blamed myself for being born, and several times I've been depressed enough to attempt suicide when I think too much about "what could've been." Because if even your own mother doesn't love or want you, how can anyone else?

I'm mature enough now to remember to take my meds even if I'm feeling good at the time, and I see a psychiatrist and a counselor regularly. You could say I've sort of grown out of my "craziness." I still offer my advice too much; I still love chocolate too much; I still worry about losing weight, but not too much.

After fifty, you take life a lot less seriously. Not that it doesn't matter; it's just that you're too tired to worry about silly stuff anymore. After fifty-five, you judge less and care more. You realize the life ahead of you is shorter than what you have behind you. You just don't want to live the drama anymore.

I feel I've lived through a lot and I'm still standing—although I sit more than I stand these days. But it's okay. I have great friends, great kids, great grandkids, and a great partner.

I've learned lessons, both good and bad. It depended on who gave the advice. Sometimes my mother gave good advice. She made me strong and I always land on my feet.

I forgive but I don't forget. Does that mean I haven't really forgiven? I'm not sure. All I know is, when my mother died

Mother, can you hear me now?

on Christmas Day a few years ago, I did the only thing I
could do: I went to work.

Mother, can you hear me now?

Acknowledgments

I would like to thank God and New Life church.

I would like to dedicate this book to my children and grandchildren.

To Tabitha and Lucy who gave me ideas when I was having a case of "Writer's block" and for being great friends through it all.

To Carol Coulter who taught both English and life thus enhancing my love of writing.

To Kathleen J and Grandma J who allowed me to include them in this book and for keeping me warm at football games.

To Chris N. who was kind enough to clean, cook, give me rides, and being there whenever needed.

To Steve Eisner, Peg Moran, Amber Griffith, Athen and everyone at Woodhall Press, especially David, whose assistance and hard work helped me through this even though I knew nothing about the process.

To Ben Tanzer for marketing me so well.

Most of all to my best friend, love of my life and soul mate, Marsha A. Bennett. She gave me a "new life" and the courage to go on through it all.

About the Author

Emory Easton is a writer and mother based in Illinois where she lives with her partner of thirty-five years. *Mother, Can You Hear Me Now?* is her debut memoir that tackles the abuse she endured as a child and the love she rediscovered as an adult.

www.ingramcontent.com/pod-product-compliance
Lightning Source LLC
Chambersburg PA
CBHW021504090426
42739CB00007B/454